D0917287

Wasted

The Story of My Son's Drug Addiction

GARDNER WEBB COLLEGE LIBRARY

WASTED

By WILLIAM CHAPIN

McGRAW-HILL BOOK COMPANY

New York • St. Louis • San Francisco

Copyright © 1972 by William Chapin. All rights reserved. Printed in the United States of America. No part of this publication may be reproduced, stored in a retrieval system, or transmitted, in any form or by any means, electronic, mechanical, photocopying, recording, or otherwise, without prior written permission of McGraw-Hill Book Company.

Library of Congress Catalog Card Number: 71–38812

07–010535–9

First Edition

DESIGNED AT THE INKWELL STUDIO

HV
5831
.C2
C47

This book is for Mark

Wasted

Prologue

MARK HAS GONE AGAIN, vanished, disappeared; will be gone for an indeterminate length of time. Mark is trying to cut himself clear of the wreckage he helped to make. He left only a few minutes ago.

Mark's departure point was his own home, a place that sits on a hill above San Francisco Bay. But that doesn't matter, it doesn't really matter—he could have gone from a hospital ward or a doctor's office or a classroom or a hippie's seamy pad on the waterfront. Nor does his destination matter. He doesn't care. For it is the act of going that counts with Mark. This is his expression, his crying out, his pain, his sorrow, his rage, his freedom—the freedom that he yearns for and that he fears.

His act of going counts with us too, his mother and father. Mark knows that, covets that knowledge, nourishes it.

Why are there nicely framed photographs of Mark's older sister in this comfortable house, but none of Mark?

1

It seems to me, Mark's father, that I can remember the features of his back better than the features of his face. This should not be so. I should not know my own son's back so well. But he is always going away from me. Rarely have we held each other, looked into each other's eyes, embraced as father and son. And even these few moments have been joyless. Grief brought us together, or agony.

No, it is not his face but his back that I forever see—in my dreams, in my conscience. His back is curved, in a thin defensive arc; he is hunched against the enemy. Against me. His hands are thrust deep in his pockets; his fingers are long and birdlike—they make uncertain motions and are better off hidden. His trousers are low, without a belt, ragged, barely kept aloft by his hips. He doesn't care. His tasseled leather jacket is streaked with food, egg yolk, coffee; it hasn't been cleaned for months. He doesn't care. His feet, encased in secondhand desert boots, are floppy, as if attached to his legs by inadequate wires. He shuffles down an endless, nameless street—endless because he cannot find what he is searching for, nameless because a name tends to fix a person in time and space and Mark does not want to be fixed in time and space; he prefers to float.

But what is he searching for, along that street? Now and then, when I am very low, I think he is searching for the ultimate escape, a quiet darkness. Now and then, when I am very low and very angry, I wish he would find it. But his is a slow way, such a slow, slow way; and the regrettable fact is that you take people with you, the voyage is not alone.

Perhaps that is what my son wants—to take people with him.

If (again) he fails to find the ultimate escape, he will return. It may be in a day or so, or in a week, or even in a month; there is no predicting when. But hunger will do it. After he has been rejected by "The Street," and by his friends, and by the girls who sometimes shelter him, physical hunger will bring him to his home on the hill. My God, what a familiar, wretched sound—the shuffle of his dirty feet on the front stairs at ten o'clock at night, the resentful vigil ended (again); and then he will be at the door with a vague, distant "hello," and then into the kitchen to grab from the refrigerator a piece of cheese or cold meat, anything, and chew on it, tear it up with his teeth like an animal. And he will mumble, his mouth full of food. He will mumble about how "the wallpaper got all folded up into bundles in Abby's room" or how "I saw two tree branches walk into the bay and sink."

What in Christ's name is he talking about? If you ask him, he says, "Never mind."

Mark has consumed drugs in large quantities. No one, including Mark, can say how much, over the years, but certainly enough to mess up his head, to rearrange the cells in his head. He's crazy. I have to say it, to write it down, to grind it into my own awareness, to accept it: he's crazy. I cannot know whether he will remain crazy, and neither can a regiment of medical men.

Mark, though, believes with an unshakable firmness that the people who have not consumed drugs in large quantities are crazier than he is. Maybe he is right; but his convictions make it difficult to argue with him about drugs. And argue with him I have, never-ending, circular arguments. Mark, oh Mark my son, *why* did you take all that dope, *why* did you blow all that pot, *why* did you drop all that acid, *why* did you flash on all that speed? To say nothing of the casual, experimental cinnamon sticks, the "reds" and the "yellows" and all the other nice little lethal bits of shit that if put into your hand went straight into your mouth.

Tell me, Mark, did you ever try heroin? I have asked you that before, but did you ever try it? Not that it makes much difference now.

The questions lie unanswered. But then, Mark's young and horrible life has been full of questions without answers. Did I fail him, did his mother, did the world, or did he fail himself? No one really knows, for sure. It is appropriate, that *questioning* curve of his back as he hunches over to protect himself against everyone—against fathers, mothers, doctors, teachers, cops, girls, boys—as he hides his sweet, vulnerable face in the curve of his body and shuffles down the street again to nowhere.

Mark is almost twenty-one years old.

Chapter 1

Mark o'hara chapin was born on a warm, sunlit day, August 5, 1949, in City Hospital, Worcester, Massachusetts. He arrived at 10:56 A.M. with a minimum of fuss. The distinguishing feature of Mark's birth was its lack of trauma, either physical or emotional.

He arrived by virtue of the Grantly Dick Read method of natural childbirth, a method fervently adopted by my wife, whose delivery of our first child, two years before, had been long and painful. Natural childbirth worked. It worked so well that Mark did not miss by very much being born in a taxicab. The time between Mark's admission to the hospital and his emergence from the womb was sufficient, and no more, for me to eat a bacon-and-eggs breakfast and read one copy of *Life* magazine. A few minutes beyond an hour.

Then the nurse called me and I saw Mark for the first time from the corridor side of a plate glass window.

I was struck by his beauty and his completeness. He was well formed. He had no cuts or bruises.

He had red hair, an impressive thatch of it, and his skin was pink and unblemished. He slept. Later, when he opened his eyes, they were a fine pure blue. He was serene, having made a marvelous commencement, self-satisfied.

I saw my wife, who was happy, healthy, comfortable, and full of praise for her obstetrician and for Dr. Grantly Dick Read; then I went home to inform our daughter Pennell that she had a baby brother and I had a son. Within six days mother and son were discharged from the hospital and came home.

We named him Mark because we thought it had an elegant sound (a trace of "old New England family" snobbishness lay there). We middle-named him O'Hara because we thought it had a rakish sound and because we wished to recall my wife's Irish father, who was many years dead. O'Hara, too, was the name by which I addressed my wife, Eleanor O'Hara Fontaine Chapin.

So Mark, to begin with, was an untroubled infant with a name like his mother's. But the world around him —that is, the immediate world of his parents—was troubled. There were tensions in the house, and a brand new infant can be affected by these. They are contagious.

If I am to try to understand Mark, I must understand the tensions that could be traced to O'Hara and me—and to our backgrounds.

In some ways, O'Hara and I were alike, perhaps too much alike. We were in our early thirties, good-looking, intelligent, politically liberal, and neurotic. She had gone to McGill University in Montreal and I to Dartmouth College in Hanover, New Hampshire. Throughout our college years we had slept together when proximity permitted it and then, with the military draft a conscious threat, had married in June, 1941. I was a cub reporter

on the *Rutland Herald* in Vermont. I proposed to O'Hara
by sending her an enormous box of chocolates, a way
that was "traditional" in her sorority. O'Hara phoned to
say how pleased she was and to ask if I really meant it and
I said yeah, I guessed I really meant it. We had a hasty
ceremony in the office of a Rutland County justice of the
peace.

Of course, one of the reasons we got married was to
escape our families—but it was vain to try. O'Hara
brought with her the conventions of a Catholic home,
even though she had fled from a school run by nuns and
called herself a renegade Catholic. Her mother, Clare,
was extremely devout, a resolute homemaker who married
Arthur Fontaine, a wealthy French-Canadian business-
man, a few years after James O'Hara's death. Despite the
surface conventions, however, the union of Arthur and
Clare was not a placid one; they communicated by bicker-
ing; and O'Hara as a girl did not regard her home as a
placid haven. And I brought with me the strictures and
sexual prurience of New England Puritanism, even
though I called myself a renegade Puritan. My mother
and father hardly communicated at all. There were long
silences in our home.

I also brought with me a sense, bestowed on me by my
mother, that I was O'Hara's intellectual and social superior. I was the "tutor," she the student. I could tell
her about Tolstoy or quote the *Communist Manifesto.*
After our marriage I realized begrudgingly that O'Hara
was just as bright as I was and tougher in the mind. Not
only that, she could jitterbug and I couldn't dance worth
a damn.

The marriage, whatever its motivations, whatever its
strengths and weaknesses—and it had both—did not
delay my induction. To avoid being an infantryman, I
joined the Army Air Corps in March, 1942, and went off
to war.

I had a bad World War II, and in 1949, the year of

Mark's birth, I still felt its impact. My younger brother, whom I loved, had died at sea, the destruction of a talented pianist and composer. I had been first a meteorologist and then a bomber pilot. Shot down over Yugoslavia, I lost my right leg and spent six months in a prisoner-of-war camp. Now, several years later, it hurt me to walk on an ill-fitting artificial limb, and I dreamt of airplanes falling from the sky.

O'Hara was repelled and attracted by the idea of suicide. She was afraid she might one day stick her head in a gas-filled oven. After months of indecision, she tried psychotherapy. She chose a psychiatrist whose office, German accent, and clothes combined to make him look the perfect product of Central Casting. His interpretation of Freud was literal: the landscape around him swarmed with penises and vaginas. He helped O'Hara in a superficial way. She used to pop out of bed in the middle of the night and write down her dreams. He interpreted the dreams, and that was her "therapy."

I went to this psychiatrist too. O'Hara was afraid of suicide. I was afraid (the most popular American male syndrome) that I might be a latent homosexual. After four sessions the doctor told me I had every reason to suspect myself of being a latent homosexual. I stopped seeing him. I don't believe he helped me at all. What helped me was to read by chance Jean-Paul Sartre's definition of a homosexual as a person who practiced homosexuality. I didn't, so that was that.

I hated my job and grumbled about it chronically. I was a copy boy editor on the *Worcester Gazette*. I hated getting up in the dark at 5 A.M. and trying to fit my wooden leg to my stump in a way that would reduce the pain of walking. I walked with my teeth clenched. The only incentive for going to work was the money—sixty dollars a week. There was no challenge; the *Gazette* was a journalistic atrocity. The depth of its publisher's thinking can be measured by the single question he put to me when we were introduced: "Do you spit on the sidewalk, young man?" I said, "No, sir." He said it was a pleasure to welcome me to the staff. My boss, the chief copy editor, was of the same order. He raged against his subordinates if they failed to correct a misspelling, but he didn't care if they hacked a good story to pieces with their pencils.

O'Hara didn't like her job either. She did the usual things: cooked, cleaned the house, washed the clothes, and cared for our daughter Pennell, and now for Mark too. She did them well; but she is a small woman and the chores left her perpetually tired.

Worcester itself was an uninspiring city. The only reason we had moved there was to dredge up a little more weekly money than I had dredged up in Vermont working for the *Rutland Herald*. Worcester had corrupt politicians and petty gangsters, but the real power resided with a score of industrial captains whose only principle was never to betray their own class for less than, say, a million dollars. Many of these men were anti-Semitic and anti-labor. The *Worcester Gazette* supported them, licked their expensive boots.

O'Hara and I lived in a $10,000 house that faced a dusty unpaved street at the summit of a hill. For entertainment we went to the movies, to concerts at the Worcester Art Museum, and to meetings of the American Veterans Committee, from which most, if not all, of our friends were drawn. I drank a fair amount.

The city, the job, the home, the marriage—all of them generated tensions, and surely some of these tensions were felt by our infant son.

He behaved as though he felt them. For he cried a lot, suffered from colic, and was a light and testy sleeper. This is not to say he wasn't ever cheerful—he also laughed a lot as soon as he learned to laugh. He had a nice round gurgle I enjoyed listening to. His emotions were close to the surface. He seemed like a coiled spring, ready to snap. When he did snap, it might give him a sense of release or it might, unpredictably, frustrate him.

The business of bottle-feeding Mark at 2 A.M. is my earliest entrenched memory of my relationship with him, a memory that would come back in later years when I tried to accommodate him and failed. Over and over again, a 2 A.M. failure. I would insinuate the bottle into his mouth; he would suck in the milk and close his eyes. I would remove the bottle like a demolition expert defusing a most delicate bomb, and start slowly toward the door. I'd never make it. Mark would screw up his face and scream. What an ungrateful and annoying little bastard I thought he was.

He began to walk when he was eleven months old, and his steps were firm and resolute. He showed no timidity, as Pennell had. He just decided that crawling was insufficient to his needs, stood up, and walked. Soon after this he ran. The second floor of our Worcester house had a long narrow hallway. I sat at one end of it, legs apart. Mark, naked, ran pell-mell to the far wall, hit it, fell down, got up and raced back into my arms. He loved this game, insisted on playing it every evening.

While still an infant, Mark feared and resented confinement. So does everyone, I suppose, but not to the extent that he did. I'm certain he was never locked in a closet and I doubt that he was ever locked in a room, but any kind of restriction put him in a rage. Nor did he like to be encumbered by clothes. Small toys, building blocks, and bottles were meant to be thrown away. It did not please him to be thrust into a high chair, or to have the hinged wooden tray brought down, like a gate, in front of him. What did please him was to toss his cereal bowl on the floor and watch O'Hara retrieve it so he could toss it again. One day O'Hara, totally exasperated, turned a bowl of oatmeal upside down on Mark's head. Mark thought that was fine; he liked the sensation of oatmeal trickling past his ears, and he started doing it himself.

Mark, even then, regarded his own body as a sort of prison he had to break out of. And thought that possessions like plastic bowls and spoons had to be got rid of, so they wouldn't slow him down.

He was capable of tremendous temper tantrums. If no one was around to frustrate Mark, then he frustrated himself. One of his first snapshots shows him lying on the sidewalk in front of the house, his face contorted. If the picture could be animated, Mark would be deliberately banging his head on the concrete. Self-induced pain. I've forgotten the provocation, but in all likelihood he had chosen an inconvenient time to wander off and had been restrained.

He was always wandering off, down the street, into the underbrush, into strangers' houses. With him usually was Brucie, a cocker spaniel who had been with us since the war days.

We worried, of course, that he would get lost, would fall into a hole, would drown in a nearby pond. We worried that he would be carried away, if for no other reason than that he was a beautiful baby. Once, reacting to that worry, I built a ridiculous playpen in the back yard. Its bars were long two-by-fours, and it was strong enough to hold a heifer. Unfortunately, I did not take into consideration the fact that Mark was not a heifer and could climb. So the routine went like this: Mark was dressed in his snowsuit and placed in the pen for an afternoon of fresh air. With him were placed many fascinating toys. Mark cried, threw out the toys, climbed over the top, and fell to freedom. Mark stopped crying and threw the toys back into the pen, imprisoning *them*. Mark, heavy in his snowsuit, waddled down the street.

Despite these alarums and excursions, Mark made it through the winter. Indeed, he made it better than O'Hara and I did; we were having a rough time. The weather was miserable, and we both had chronic colds. I slipped and slithered on the icy sidewalks trying to keep my wooden leg under me. O'Hara complained about being exhausted; I complained about putting chains on tires so I could

drive home from a thankless job. We argued over trivialities. I think we both felt trapped by our children, rather
than fulfilled by them; and I think both of us wondered,
without daring to put it into words, whether this marriage
was worth saving.

An incident during supper stands out as typical of the
way O'Hara and I abused our relationship. I cut my finger
with a carving knife and blood flowed freely. Before we
could get a bandage on the cut, I managed to walk into
every room on the first floor, leaving spatters of blood
behind me. This got O'Hara mad—she couldn't understand why I didn't sit still and bleed in one place, as any
sensible person would. And her attitude got *me* mad: how
unreasonable she was to react like this, while I was
wounded. To get even, I stomped out of the house holding
my finger high, and obeying a sudden zany impulse, went
to a prizefight. I sat glumly in a ringside seat (having
squandered money on a top ticket didn't make me feel
any better), and after the fights I drove home. O'Hara
had mopped the floor and done the dishes, and she was no
longer mad. We started to laugh. The ability to laugh at
ourselves—that is what made the marriage worth saving; or at least it saved the marriage.

One morning in March, while it was still dark and a
slow rain was freezing as it hit the ground, O'Hara and I
sat in the kitchen drinking coffee before I left for my
6 A.M. date with the *Worcester Gazette*. We were depressed and silent. What a way to live, I was thinking.
When O'Hara finally spoke, she said, "Bill, why don't we
try California?"

Over the years, that had been one of O'Hara's favorite
requests to which I had always said no. She had never
been to California, but it was far away, and for her its
distance must have held the promise of a solution.

"All right," I said, "we'll try California. By God, we
will."

Chapter 2

It was october, 1951, and Mark was two years and three months old. I accepted the first job offer I received, which was from the *Oakland Tribune*. But our goal was San Francisco, the magical city, rather than Oakland; so I searched for a place to rent on the San Francisco side of the bay while O'Hara remained in Worcester to sell off our property.

I found a place in a tract called Broadmoor Village, for $105 a month. On the day I signed the lease I stood before a picture window (every house in Broadmoor had a picture window) and looked across the entire city of San Francisco to the towers of the Golden Gate Bridge. The view was beautiful and exciting and my hopes were high. On the day I drove O'Hara and the children from the airport to Broadmoor Village the fog was so thick that O'Hara stood before the same picture window and tried to see what lay beyond the back yard fence.

It was a lesson to be learned, that fog. O'Hara learned

that she could travel 3,000 miles in pursuit of the sun and still be denied it except on special days. I learned that I could drive home drunk late at night and be unable to distinguish one garage from another. In the fog they all looked alike.

The house itself was almost empty when O'Hara and the children moved in. We had almost no money, so it stayed empty for months. Our shoes clattered noisily on the hardwood floors. But I bought some hand tools, bought Japanese birch, and set about making furniture that was less graceful than it was strong. Furniture-making kept me busy every afternoon. I liked doing it but I was slow. O'Hara, meanwhile, dressed Pennell and Mark in their same old snowsuits and put them outside to play.

Predictably, Mark established himself in the neighborhood much more rapidly than Pennell did. He roamed the street, cheerfully banging on doors. At first, Pennell's one and only close friend was a tiger-striped kitten, a stray she adopted and named Tinker. The kitten turned into a cat and lived with us for twelve years.

One day we had a door-to-door photographer take pictures of the children, "kiddy portraits" to be sent to the folks back East. The incident reflected in a glaring way the differences between our daughter and our son.

Dressed in their best, the children sat on a couch. Their clothes were festive, the atmosphere was not. The photographer, a thin youth with a sparrow's face, pranced in front of his subjects. Apparently he had been instructed that clowning was the best way to put the kiddies at ease. But his reflex camera with its enormous snout of a lens, swinging heavily from the strap around his neck, resembled a weapon.

"Hey there, Penny! Wanna see me do a Howdy Doody? How's that one, Penny? And you too, Sonny. Did you like that one too?"

Click went the camera. Click, click. Fast talk, fast laughter, and the constant click of the camera.

Pennell did not like the camera or its bearer or his version of Howdy Doody. She shrank deeper and deeper into the couch, her hands buried between her legs, her mouth clamped shut. To Mark, though, the clowning was a challenge. He could be even funnier. He laughed, he shrieked, he stood on his head, he did somersaults, he tried literally to drag his sister into the photographic arena. For me the scene was endless.

We got the pictures all right, cheap prints at cheap prices, and we did send them to the folks back East. They showed Mark in a state of happy hysteria; they showed Pennell with fear in her eyes and tears on her cheeks. They said more than I thought this photographer could say.

Mark's first exposure to school occurred while we lived in Broadmoor Village. It was a nursery class taught by the plump and motherly wife of the Village's Presbyterian minister. There were cookies and crayons, beads and blocks. No doubt there were prayers too, but it was a relief to O'Hara to get the children out of the house. Mark was an active participant in the classes, Pennell a passive one; and Mark outdid himself at the "graduation ceremonies." Ever curious, unable to sit still, he slipped away from O'Hara while the teacher was in the midst of a farewell chat to pupils and parents. He climbed the stage, went straight to the piano, and began to play a series of small but intrusive noises. The teacher chose to ignore him. But Mark was not to be ignored, and as inspiration took him from one end of the keyboard to the other, more and more members of the audience broke up and the graduation ceremonies fell apart. Everybody went home.

Walking up the street, O'Hara, exasperated, gave Mark several swipes across the legs with the stick from a toy balloon. It was impulsive, trivial punishment, and in the context of the entire day amusing. Or so I thought, and I described it all to my mother in my next letter to the East. Her reply was astonishing: she said that if we disciplined Mark like a member of the Gestapo, he would grow up to be a member of the Gestapo. In my view, a great number of my mother's reactions to events were political, doctrinaire, and blind. I wrote back straight-away, saying that her conclusions were bullshit.

I doubt that Mark was traumatized by that balloon stick. But later, as an adolescent, he accused both O'Hara and me of spanking him needlessly and too often. Invari-ably he contrasted his upbringing with the methods used at Summerhill, the British school made famous by its ex-treme permissiveness. For years, A. S. Neill's book about Summerhill was Mark's gospel.

A psychologist once told me that in his complaining about too many spankings, Mark was actually seeking out more discipline, was asking for a stronger father. Maybe so. I just don't know. I do know that I still retain a measure of guilt that is tied to my handling of Mark as a child. I feel especially guilty about one terrible day when I struck Mark on the face. He and Pennell had been put to bed in the early evening. Some people were due to drop by for drinks, and I was tense and tired and had already consumed a couple of martinis. The children refused to calm down; they kept throwing things at each other. I leaned over Mark, close to him, and ordered him to go to sleep. It would have made as much sense to order him to stand at attention and salute the flag; he was full of energy and excitement. As I spoke, he spit, and I hit him with the back of my right hand. He must have been stunned by pain and fright, for he didn't even cry. My knuckles had cut his face, and when O'Hara saw him she could only say, "What in the world did you do to Mark?" I couldn't answer; I felt awful.

There were many changes in the next few years. It wasn't a stable life, but neither was it dull.

In the fall of 1952 I switched from the *Oakland Tribune* copy desk to the San Francisco *Chronicle* copy desk. No longer did I have to rise at 5 A.M. to drive to Oakland and sit beside a 300-pound copyreader who ate chocolate marshmallow cookies. Instead I worked at night, had a quick and joyless affair with a newspaperwoman, and drank in a bar almost every morning from one to two. Often the drinking would continue in someone's apartment until the sun came up. I used to hate driving home after the birds had started to sing; their songs accused me; but I kept on doing it.

I worked for the *Chronicle* fifteen years. The paper demanded a kind of boy-scout loyalty that all of us at one time or another found oppressive. The compensations, however, were great. The paper was intelligent and lively; the people I worked for were also intelligent and lively. They were curious about many things, and did not take themselves too seriously. We on the editorial staff were somewhat clannish; we worked together and played together. These people remain among my closest friends.

Most of my friends lived in Marin County, the affluent and beautiful territory north of the Golden Gate Bridge. It was, and is, a homing place for young executives, swingers, artists, writers, and newspapermen, so it seemed inevitable that we should move there too, and we did. In January, 1953, we dumped our household goods into a U-Haul trailer and drove to the Marin town of Mill Valley, where I had rented another tract house for $105 a month. This tract was older than Broadmoor Village and bore a less pretentious name. It was called Goheen Gulch, because a man named Goheen developed it and a muddy sluggish creek ran through it during the wet season.

Mark loved that creek. Almost daily he wandered down there, played under a bridge, got himself covered with mud, and wandered home again. We worried about it, and spanked him a few times, but this did not keep him away from the creek.

Our residence in Goheen Gulch had a temporary feeling, even more than the one in Broadmoor. I continued to build furniture (this was becoming therapy as well as carpentry), but now it was furniture for our next dwelling; we aspired to rise above the level of a tract house. Indeed, we had ambitious and unrealistic plans.

Touring Marin County, we soon discovered the Belvedere Lagoon. To us it seemed the very essence of California living—swimming, sunlight, sailing, cocktails on the elegant redwood deck—and we resolved to live nowhere else. We borrowed money from my father and purchased for $6,000 a lot with a sixty-foot frontage on the lagoon. There, in time, would stand our dream house.

The idea, never carefully thought out, was that I would build the dream house, since we could not possibly afford it otherwise. We found a young and sympathetic architect, Henry Schubart, who submitted preliminary drawings that everyone agreed were exactly right for us. They weren't right, however. They were wrong for us, because they laid great stress on "family togetherness," via a huge all-purpose room and scarcity of doors. If O'Hara and I had been honest with ourselves and each other, we would have admitted that we did not want to spend that much intimate time with the kids.

Henry Schubart was a slow and conscientious architect, which was fortunate, because it gave O'Hara and me a number of months to brood about the dream house, and to come at last to the painful knowledge that I was never going to build it, that I did not have enough skill and determination to build an entire house, and that it was absurd to assume that a newspaperman's wages would permit him to live on the Belvedere Lagoon. It was a wild, fantastical scheme, that dream house.

But it took a while to learn this, and the learning was not easy, since it meant accepting defeat and retrenchment. It meant heavier drinking and more staying out late after work, and eventually it meant that I fell prey to an overwhelming anxiety. This got so bad that I went to a psychiatrist, not frivolously, as I had in Worcester, but with a real sense of urgency and need. My psychiatrist, Dr. Bernard Kahn, was employed by the Kaiser Health

Plan, which I belonged to, so my fifty-minute sessions cost only five dollars each. A bargain.

Dr. Kahn had a difficult time getting me to talk about what mattered. I used his Jewishness to delay the inevitable. I would lie on the psychiatric couch, stiff as a board, and send out a feeler.

"What if inside me I'm secretly anti-Semitic?"

Silence.

"What if I've got all those Jewish friends just to conceal my anti-Semitism?"

Silence, a heavy silence.

"What if I started to free-associate and all of a sudden I called out 'kike'? That would really bother me, it really would."

Finally, Dr. Kahn said, "For Christ's *sake*, Mr. Chapin, when are you going to stop this nonsense and get going?"

Eventually I did stop the nonsense and Dr. Kahn helped me. He was tough, and he wouldn't let me play games. He showed me that emotions rather than logic would almost always shape my life, and that I was sometimes self-destructive. But he also showed me that these patterns were true of many people, and that I should not let them bedevil me. Accept yourself, he said, and in many ways I did, even if I could not always know myself.

During my last visit, Dr. Kahn advised me not to switch jobs without consulting him. He didn't say why and I didn't ask. But it was wise advice, which I failed to follow. Twenty years later it is easy to see that he was telling me not to rock the boat because a new job might swamp me.

Dr. Kahn is dead now. He was a good man who did not believe in perfectibility. The one thing about him that puzzled me was his atrocious taste in literature: he loved potboilers.

While I was seeing Dr. Kahn I went, dreading it, to Henry Schubart's architectural offices and told him to stop drawing plans. I mentioned psychotherapy, the accumulation of too many pressures, my financial fears. Henry said he was very sorry and sent me a modest bill. Within a month we sold our lot on the lagoon for $6,000 (we could have got $50,000 if we had held it for ten years) and bought a house in Sausalito. The longest parties and the heaviest drinking were there, and I wanted to be there too.

Sausalito—that expensive, beautiful, high-living village on San Francisco Bay—had almost nothing in the way of organized recreation for children. I welcomed this; I, for one, was not going to let my kids be regimented.

We moved to Sausalito, to the house we still live in, on December 14, 1954. Mark was five years old, Pennell seven. Their rooms, in the house where they were to grow up, were on an upper floor. There were no other rooms on that level—only a cubicle containing a toilet but no washbowl. The children had both privacy and isolation— a condition that made for intense rivalry and, later, intense affection. For years we were to hear Pennell screaming at Mark, "Get out of my room, get out of my room!" Then, one day, the screaming stopped.

The rest of the house had an eccentric charm of sorts, an unexpected sequence of rooms, an agreeable clutter. I, rather than O'Hara, chose to buy it, and often she referred to it as an "overgrown cottage." She desired a house with more stature, a place that would command respect.

Much of my spare time away from the *Chronicle* was occupied with trying to give the house more stature. The do-it-yourself projects were endless: putting on a sundeck, adding a room, building kitchen cabinets, landscaping the front yard, building fences. But I did not occupy myself very much with the children. They went their own ways. Soon they were enrolled in the Sausalito public schools, but I never joined the PTA ("a bourgeois waste of time"), never went to a school board meeting, and only once or twice conferred with teachers. I had a ready excuse, of course: my night hours on the newspaper.

My rationale for letting the children go their own ways was that I wished to encourage their individualism, and I felt that Sausalito, with its loose, easygoing manners, was the ideal place for this. I don't think I gave Mark and Pennell enough to hang on to. There was no steady, unspoken authority.

Now and then, pushed by vague feelings of guilt, I tried to change this separation of father and children. I took both of them to the tennis courts and discovered that I lacked the necessary patience; I got bored with shagging tennis balls. I played pitch-and-catch with Mark in front of the house. I took him to an occasional football or baseball game.

I took Mark fishing. Once, when he was eight, I woke him at 3 A.M., as soon as I got home from work. We drove off in the darkness so that we could reach a stream before dawn. It was the fishing season's opening day, and the streams were certain to be crowded. Sitting beside me in the station wagon, Mark was happy and excited. We had fixed our breakfast together, with nobody else; we were sitting here together, with nobody else, and I believe we both had a sense of rare and secret comradeship, of a benign conspiracy.

I parked on a dirt road near Conn Creek, which flows out of Lake Hennessey above the Napa Valley. It was starting to get light. We found a shallow pool that was fed by fast water running over rocks. Mark was all action, darting here and there, talking and laughing. I told him to slow down lest he spook the fish. I rigged his rod and my own and baited the hooks with salmon eggs. Mark, barefoot, waded into the fast water and dropped his line into the pool. Within seconds he had a strike. He gave a swift, convulsive pull with both hands; the fish, flashing in the early light, flew over his head and plopped into the water behind him. He was in a frenzy of delight. "I got one, I got one, I got one!" He thrashed around in the stream. Unbelievably, the fish stayed on the line and I got my net to it and removed the hook. It was a nine-inch rainbow that to Mark must have been a giant. It was wonderful to see him so happy, so triumphant. We had, then, on that small stream, several moments of shared ecstasy that have never been duplicated. And that I feel sure never will be.

Both of us caught a few more fish, none of them as large as Mark's first one. We ate an early lunch in the warm sun and started home about noon. I was sleepy, having had no sleep the night before, so I parked off the highway and napped in the back of the station wagon. I was very content. It was a nice day with my son. Back home, Mark repeatedly told O'Hara that it was he, not Dad, who had caught the biggest fish. He ate his biggest fish for breakfast the following morning.

But it was seldom like that.

Mark, I told myself, did not mind, did not miss my companionship. He had a quality of insouciance, and in Sausalito, as he always had been elsewhere, he was cheerful, curious, and outgoing. He had friends in every other house on the block. He explored the entire town; he spent hours in a wooded glen; he made tree houses; he pestered me for a rifle and I bought him an air pistol; he stole a guinea pig from a children's zoo in San Francisco and I made him take it back. School was too easy; he was a complete reader by the time he was seven, with an amazing vocabulary. With his quick smile, his freckled face, and his bright red hair, he was beautiful to look at, and other parents found him enormously appealing.

Once, a few months after we moved to Sausalito, I distinguished myself by getting arrested for drunkenness. I had closed a downtown bar on the waterfront at 2 A.M. and a patrol car picked me up while I was trying to stagger home. I spent the night in a jail cell. The next morning O'Hara and some of our friends bailed me out. By the time I was safely home in my own living room, the arrest was already being turned into a legend, something

I could later use repeatedly for a laugh and for its shock value. Mark and a couple of his pals bounced into the living room while we were sitting there. He hardly looked at me as he roared past, toward his own room.

"Hi, Dad," he shouted, "how's jail?"

Chapter 3

Mark went from kindergarten to elementary school with no signs of becoming a super-achiever; his grades were good, his attitude toward his teachers was casual and unworried. He had a tendency to get into mild trouble, but he was neither mean nor vicious. He pulled a fire alarm box near our house and hid in the woods when the big red engine charged up the hill; he bloodied a smaller boy's nose for the sheer excitement of it, and got punished; he broke a balloon full of water on the floor of his bedroom, and this time it was O'Hara, not Mark, who had the temper tantrum.

Now and then he announced that he was going to run away. O'Hara would say, "All right," and give him some cookies in a red handkerchief tied to a stick. He would then leave, but he always came back in a few hours.

He could be responsible too. He rescued a cat that was being dramatically hanged in a garage by a child with a childish streak of sadism. Mark cut the cat down while some other boys, petrified, stood by.

Above all, Mark seemed happy and buoyant.

During these years he developed to a high degree his ability to argue. He preferred to argue with O'Hara, perhaps because she was more readily available, perhaps because he felt she was a worthier opponent than I. The arguments usually took place in the kitchen while supper was being prepared.

"Mom, can I save up my allowance and buy a gun? Would that be OK?"

"You're really not old enough to have a gun, Mark."

"Alex has a gun."

"I know but I guess Pat and Dick feel differently about it, that's all. Besides, we just don't think you'd have any place to shoot it around here. Too many people."

"I could shoot it up on Wolfback Ridge."

"Mark, your father's told you . . . a gun is too dangerous at your age. Now please let me get supper."

"Now just a minute, Mom. Just a minute."

"OK, what is it?"

"Is my allowance my money?"

"Yes, it's yours."

"Then why can't I spend it on what I want?"

"Well, it's yours within *reason*. But we're still responsible for—"

"Now just a minute, Mom. Just a *minute*."

"Oh Mark, please just knock it off for now, will you?"

And so it went, a daily ritual. He argued for the sake of argument, about abstractions as well as guns: "Would I be better than other people if I had three eyes and they only had one? Would I, Mom?"

His arguments with me were not only less frequent but less prolonged, since I could not or would not tolerate them as well as O'Hara did. And as Mark grew older, our conversations dwindled into laconic exchanges, comments, instructions, routine questions and answers.

"How was school today, Mark?"

"Fine."

"Hi, Mark, what are you up to?"

"Nothing much."

"Want to go for a ride in the car?"

"Mmm, OK."

Mark must have sensed that, challenged by his verbal facility, I feared defeat. And by manipulating that fear he could get me very angry.

Once, after six hours of remodeling our kitchen, I was resting on my bed feeling sorry for myself because I had to leave for the *Chronicle* in an hour. Mark came in, school books under an arm, and asked if he could go downtown. There was no reason why he shouldn't, but I was out of sorts and like a fool said, "No, you can't." His reply was to mumble a few words I took to be provocative and head for the door.

"What did you say?"

"Never mind."

"Come back here and say that again!"

"Never mind."

"Don't you 'never mind' me, goddammit!"

I was off the bed in an instant, climbing all over him. I didn't swing my fist; I shook him as a dog shakes a cat, and he cried. His books fell from his grasp and we felt disgust (both of us, I'm sure) at the way they splattered on the floor. We were demeaned.

I hated myself for jumping him; it was senseless and cruel. But I still overreact when Mark says, "Never mind," as he often does. His "Never mind" is like a disdainful yet resigned little shrug of the shoulders: why should he bother repeating himself since he knows I am not going to accept his words, or even understand them.

Considering Mark's natural curiosity, his eagerness to acquire random knowledge, one might assume that we would have discussed sex when he was a pre-adolescent. Not so. Not among the New England Chapins. Questions were asked, yes, and I think the answers were honest; but they had too much of the clinic in their tone, they failed to imply any joy or pleasure in sex, and they were above all brief. Sexual anatomy, the functions of the male and female sexual organs, sexual techniques—the explanations of these were usually given in a let's-hurry-up-and-get-this-over-with tone of anxiety. I myself had come by sexual knowledge early on, through an endless series of colloquial lectures delivered by a family of Polish boys and girls whose parents' farm adjoined ours in Vermont. I assumed Mark would be similarly educated. But it is not the best way, because it includes so much superstition and folklore. The best way is to get it straight, from parents who have a happy and consistent point of view.

I vividly recall two of Mark's comments about sex; ten years divided them, and it seems to me that the first showed more sophistication and confidence than the second.

One day when Mark was nine he referred to a "queer."

"Do you know what 'queer' means, Mark?"

"It's so nasty I don't want to talk about it."

"Oh come on. If you use the word you ought to know what it means."

"It's two boys trying to make a baby," he said.

One day when Mark was nineteen, he and I were stretched out on couches in the living room, doing nothing. "Think you'll get married, Mark?" I asked. It was an idle question—I was "making conversation" more than anything else.

"If I can learn to fuck," he said. It sounded like a put-on; but I'm sure he meant it, and I didn't ask him if I could help him learn.

In the summer of 1958, when Mark was nearly nine and ready for the fifth grade, we took an extended vacation in Japan. By this time I had been promoted to chief of the *Chronicle* copy desk. We were in the throes of a circulation war at the newspaper, the work was hectic, I was very tired, and I had a strong need to "get away." Hence Japan.

On account of my military disability, I was entitled to travel with my family aboard military ships or airplanes on a "space available" basis. To go from San Francisco to Tokyo on the *USS Breckinridge* cost us fifty-two dollars. It should have been the greatest bargain ever.

I liked Tokyo fairly well, and so did O'Hara. Pennell shrank from its strangeness, and Mark embraced it. Boys are *Ichiban* (Number One) in Japan, and this slim, nimble Caucasian with red hair and an impudent manner was repeatedly stopped on the street by admirers. He loved the attention.

But I, as usual, was anxious not to be conventional, to be exposed as a "tourist," so I insisted that we veer away from conventional paths. Through a friend who worked on the *Pacific Stars and Stripes*, I arranged for us to spend several days at a country inn on the seacoast a hundred miles southwest of Tokyo.

The inn was at Imaihama, on the Izu peninsula. It was remote, at the end of a dirt road that twisted down the rocky coastline, and it was lovely: rooms of soft gleaming wood with straw-matted floors, long quiet corridors, and a green band of pine trees and moss between the building and the beach. The inn's manager spoke with a mysterious English; the maids spoke no English at all.

On our second day at the inn Mark, already friends with everyone, played baseball on the beach with a group of boys somewhat older than he was. They made allowances for his age, and he got along fine. It was deceptively hot; the air was full of moisture, the sky veiled by a high thin overcast. Mark was on the beach until evening. When he went to bed his skin was bright pink and he was exhausted.

He woke us about midnight. He was moaning and he had vomited. He continued to vomit until he could no more than retch painfully and bring up some greenish bile. When the morning light appeared, O'Hara and I began to think, with mounting concern, of the language barrier in this Japanese inn.

We were lucky. When we got up we discovered that the inn had as a guest an American resident of Tokyo who spoke fluent Japanese. With his help we got a doctor from Shimoda, the nearest town. This man, who was gray, gentle, and stooped, out of an earlier century, took Mark's temperature. It was 102. The doctor took a huge needle from his tattered gladstone bag and gave Mark an injection of glucose, then handed us some pills. He indicated that Mark had sunstroke. Give him the pills and plenty of tea, he said. He charged us a minuscule fee and departed. We felt slightly reassured.

But Mark's retching grew worse. He was wracked by spasms, and we could keep no fluid in him. Further, our interpreter had left for Tokyo and we again felt isolated.

I managed to put through a phone call to Bill Hanway, the *Stars and Stripes* executive who had set up our trip to the inn. This led to an incredibly complex series of calls involving me, Hanway, Hanway's personal physician, a large Tokyo hospital, and a hospital in Ito, which was the closest city of any size. The calls resulted in a decision to take Mark to the Ito hospital on the grounds that he might have appendicitis. This was a long-distance and highly speculative diagnosis, but we couldn't afford to ignore it.

These negotiations consumed hours, while Mark's condition remained unchanged. By the time I was off the phone it was ten o'clock at night and a storm was blowing in off the sea. Our country inn shuddered and banged in the wind and the rain, and the lights were low. Nevertheless, we got a taxi whose driver agreed to risk the cliffside road to Ito.

We had to split up: O'Hara would take Mark to Ito, I would stay with Pennell at the inn and join them in the morning. Why didn't I, the father of the family, go to Ito? It is a father's job to face the storm, not a mother's. The rationale was that O'Hara would have less trouble with the language in Ito (an English-speaking doctor had been promised us); but I should have gone. Instead, O'Hara climbed into the taxicab at midnight and with Mark on her lap vanished down the rainswept road. I went back to our room and nursed a bottle of Scotch until dawn.

In the morning Pennell and I boarded the bus to Ito. She looked dazed and I looked bleary. I had a telephone number for the hospital, our only link to O'Hara and Mark at this stage, and at the Ito bus station I used it. A stream of Japanese words came over the line. I couldn't even say "I don't understand you" in Japanese, so I said it repeatedly in English. After an agonizing minute or two, a man who introduced himself as an American missionary took over the phone at the other end of the line and asked in a jolly top-of-the-morning-to-you voice if he could help. Was an American mother there with a sick boy, I asked. No. He was sure he would have noticed them. I said they had to be there, in Ito. He said Ito had another hospital, a second-rate establishment, and he gave me its phone number and address. Seconds later I heard O'Hara's voice.

"Bill, you've got to hurry. Where on earth *are* you?"

"We're at the bus station. What's going on?"

"This is an appalling place. I've never seen anything like it. The doctor says Mark's got appendicitis and he wants to operate right away. Please please hurry. For God's sake, hurry!"

I got a cab and we raced through narrow streets. O'Hara was waiting for me at the hospital entrance. I removed my shoes (remembering my Japanese manners), and she led me up a flight of dingy stairs. Pennell trailed along all but forgotten. Dirt was everywhere. An old woman with her arm swathed in a blood-stained bandage shuffled past us, staring. Later O'Hara told me she had seen people with running sores which no one seemed to be tending, and a single spigot of water for all the patients. Now she was crying. She said, "One time last night Mark looked at me and he said, 'Am I going to die, Mom? Am I?' "

He was lying on a mattress in the far corner of a large room. The windows' wooden shutters were closed; light came from a dusty bulb at the end of a wire. There were cobwebs, there was a box of sand (for putting out fires?), there was no furniture. Mark seemed alone and terribly small and defenseless. Why the Christ had we come on this trip to Japan?

He was drowsy and exhausted, but he opened his eyes when I knelt on the mattress and leaned over near his face. "Hi, Dad," he said, and he tried to smile.

This brought a swift rush of tears to my eyes, and I said, "Hi, Mark, you'll be all right, you're going to be all right, we'll get you out of here."

But I didn't altogether believe it, and he must have been touched by my disbelief. "Maybe I'm going to die?" he said.

A girl brought us tea. Pennell talked to Mark, fire-crackers popped and sputtered in the street outside (a celebration was in progress), and O'Hara led me into the corridor where the children couldn't hear us. She and Mark had arrived around three, she told me, and found the place was dark. She had pounded on the door and been let in by the doctor who seemed to own the hospital, and they had tried to talk to each other in sign language. Then the doctor had put Mark in the room he was in now and examined him.

"It was awful," O'Hara said. "He took his temperature with a thermometer that was just lying in a pan of dirty water with a lot of other thermometers."

O'Hara cringed as she relived her introduction to this "hospital." She told me the doctor had cut Mark's ear with a scalpel to get a blood sample. She told me the worst part of all was when two women in dirty smocks came in and gave Mark an enema. They made him stand over a slop bucket, and he was so weak they had to hold him up.

"Where's the doctor now," I asked. "What's he doing?"

"I don't know. He's gone off. But after he took the blood sample he came back with a dictionary. He pointed to a word—it was 'appendicitis'—and then he said, 'Cut, cut,' and he made cutting motions on his stomach.'"

I looked at Mark to make sure he wasn't listening to us. His eyes were closed.

"I said '*No, no!* Not 'til Papa-san comes,'" O'Hara went on. "'Wait 'til Papa-san comes.' I was getting hysterical and finally I screamed, 'If only somebody could speak *English!*' I think maybe he understood. He looked sort of startled and said, 'OK,OK,OK,' and left. I haven't seen him since."

We waited helplessly in Mark's room. None of us said very much. We wiped away the sweat, listened to the street sounds get louder, and gave water to Mark.

In the middle of the morning the doctor reappeared, with a pretty, well-dressed woman who bowed and in excellent English said, "Good morning. I am Mrs. Takahashi. I live in Ito now, but for fifteen years I lived in Seattle. Dr. Sugami asked me to come. May I be of assistance?"

"Thank God," said O'Hara. "Yes, thank you, you may be of assistance."

Dr. Sugami was a stocky, powerful-looking young man with an impassive face. We shook hands. Then, with Mrs. Takahashi translating, we discussed Mark. He said, "The boy is too sick to be moved. It is important that his appendix be removed before it bursts. Do not worry. I have done the operation many times and it is not dangerous."

I said, "I do not want you to think that my wife and I do not appreciate your medical efforts. If you do think that, then I apologize. But my wife and I want to talk to our friends in Tokyo. We would like to get an ambulance to take Mark to Tokyo. If that can't be done, we will try to get a Tokyo surgeon to come here and help you in the operation."

It was less than a vote of confidence, and of course Dr. Sugami knew it. He bowed stiffly and left the room. But now we had an interpreter, and we went to work again on the long-distance telephone. Every call seemed to meet obstacles, but at last we got an opinion from the chief surgeon at St. Luke's International Hospital in Tokyo: it would be reasonably safe to move Mark.

Mrs. Takahashi glanced at her watch. "A train will be leaving in five minutes," she said.

Everybody started running around. Mrs. Takahashi got us two cabs. I picked up Mark and in my stocking feet carried him downstairs, through mud puddles and past a curious crowd, to one of the cabs. Pennell grabbed my shoes. Mrs. Takahashi stayed with us. Our drivers sped to the station and I ran down the platform with Mark in my arms while O'Hara shouted, "Stop the train, stop the train!" For several terrible moments I thought Pennell had been left behind in the confusion, and it was not until the train was actually pulling out that we found her aboard.

Mrs. Takahashi insisted on staying on the train for a half-hour, and she asked the conductor to phone ahead so that an ambulance would meet us in Tokyo. Mrs. Takahashi was a superb woman.

The ambulance met us at Shimbashi, a Tokyo suburb, and drove us to St. Luke's Hospital. It was a big, ugly building. Nurses hurried up and down the corridors. The rustle of their uniforms, heavy with starch, was one of the most comforting sounds I have ever heard.

Mark received excellent care. He did not have appendicitis. He had sunstroke, just as the gray old doctor from Shimoda had told us.

The hospital kept him under observation for five days. Soon after his discharge, we sailed for San Francisco, and Mark was himself again, outwardly cheerful and noisy. But deep within him, I suspect, he had undergone a significant change as a result of his falling ill in that country inn at Imaihama. It was the smallest of shadows, at first. But he now saw the possibility of death at an age when most children see only the possibility of life. In the next several years there would be an occasional pause in his cheerfulness, and he would ask questions such as, "What's it like to die?"

Chapter 4

MARK'S ILLNESS was a harrowing experience for the rest of the family too, and it might have been enough to keep us away from Japan for many years. There are, after all, other countries to visit, and as a family we had never been to Europe. But it did not keep us away, and this can be explained, I believe, by a single, seemingly trivial incident.

While Mark was convalescing in the hospital we stayed in the Dai Ichi, a dull, inexpensive Tokyo hotel. One evening I mentioned to O'Hara in a deliberately offhand manner that I would like to go out alone, just to wander around. O'Hara said all right, why not? I got a cab ride to Asakusa, a large entertainment district, and I walked into the first night club I saw. As soon as I displayed some 10,000-yen bills the club manager opened his eyes wide, and seconds later a slightly overweight hostess wearing an old-fashioned Western gown sat beside me.

Nothing very exceptional happened. I drank, my hostess and I danced to the music of a pathetic little band, and we exchanged banalities in simple English. Once the girl put her hand on my knee—it seemed more a friendly gesture than a sexual one—and discovered that I wore an artificial leg. She was curious, sympathetic, and not in the least embarrassed. She was gratified that I had lost my leg over Germany rather than over Japan.

A couple of hours passed, I said goodby and left. I did not resolve, then and there, to return to Japan for a longer visit, but there was no doubt that I would. She was just an anonymous girl in an anonymous bar, and not especially pretty; but she had a gentleness, an openness, a soft allure that confirmed what little I had read about Japanese women. A curtain had been lifted for a moment on a world I wanted to know more deeply, so I would go back to Japan.

I would bring my family with me, of course, because I wanted that world too.

We returned in 1962. Before that second trip Mark moved from elementary school to junior high. It is amazing how little I remember of him during this period. I have to rely on O'Hara for the sketchiest of details. It's as though Mark had ceased to be a person to me and did not become one again until he also became a problem to me—a problem created by drugs. Before that? He was in and out of the house, constantly on the go; he rode his bicycle; he woke me up in the morning when I was trying to sleep after a late night's work; he wrangled with Pennell; he tried out for a school basketball team and, according to O'Hara, was disappointed because I did not see him play; he did a few house chores, unwillingly; he complained that his teachers were boring. That's about all. To me, Mark was a shadow child, taken for granted. I paid more attention to Pennell. We looked alike, we found it easy to talk to each other, she spent a lot more time in the house than Mark did, and I was made happy by her progress. She had lost much of the shyness that was so confining to her personality in earlier years; now she had a surprisingly lusty laugh. She was interested in acting and painting, and talented in both.

Beyond all this, Pennell was a girl.

Mark was thirteen when we flew to Japan in August, 1962. This time it was for a whole year. The *Chronicle* gave me leave (it had no choice under our union contract), and I signed on as chief of the copy desk of the *Pacific Stars and Stripes*. My primary assignment was to train copyreaders and to select a man who could take my place when I left.

Stars and Stripes was a ridiculous newspaper, a military house organ that fawned before the generals. But its staff included some fine people, and we were united by a common goal: to get the job done as quickly and easily as possible so we could turn to more important matters in the city of Tokyo. On the copy desk the prevailing topic of conversation was sex.

O'Hara and I rented a weird house—half Japanese, half Swiss chalet—in a Japanese neighborhood. It cost $280 a month, a sum that soon had us borrowing money. We enrolled the children in The American School in Japan, which was ten minutes away by bus and contained pupils from forty different nations—embassy brats, for the most part. We chose the house and the school by design, to steer clear of the American military enclaves.

Pennell hated the neighborhood in the beginning; indeed, she hated the whole business of moving to Japan. She was very homesick. Mark loved it.

He started the year typically by letting curiosity get him into trouble. Our house had a spacious lawn and a fine green garden; it also had armies of ants, and Mark decided it would be a good idea to kill them with scalding water. He heated up a kettle, took it outside, and went to work. Then he decided to test what he had read about centrifugal force. Arm extended, he swung the kettle in a full circle; the lid stayed on and the water stayed in. At least it stayed in until Mark's kettle struck the branch of a tree. The water splashed down his back and long strips of skin peeled away. But he didn't even cry; he ran into the house and stood under a cold shower. We got him to a neighborhood doctor within minutes, and the burns healed without leaving any scars.

The rest of the year was all to the good for Mark. He opened up like a strong young flower coming to bloom. He became even more receptive to new thoughts and new sensations. Tokyo is confusing, an endless sprawl of buildings and people; but it is a safe city by our standards, and Mark often traveled alone, by bus or train. We did not worry about him. He went to other boys' houses and brought his new friends home, where they would try out their appalling English on O'Hara and me. He went to Shibuya, a big shopping area, to eat in cheap noodle parlors and sit in cheap movie houses watching triple-features.

He didn't study much, nor did he have to. The American School in Japan (its antiquated facilities were used in World War II to train the Imperial Army's spies) was an odd place, but its very oddity seemed to suit Mark. Most of the teachers were in Japan for the same reason I was: to have a good time. They were unimpressed by rules. Discipline was lax, and they seldom bothered to hand out grades. But they got Mark reading things he probably would not have read in the United States, and they got him writing poetry. One of his poems showed so much sophistication for a thirteen-year-old that I gave it to Ruth Witt-Diamont, a retired English professor then living in Tokyo, who had founded the Poetry Center at San Francisco State College. She thought the poem was promising and encouraged Mark to continue. Here is his first poem:

> Who knows what happened then?
> It is only the memory of man,
> And in the future there is nothing to find,
> Except the imagination of mankind.

Who is sure of what will come?
Only if we judge the past
Can we guess the future.

One of Mark's teachers, ostensibly teaching a course in geometry, spent all his classroom hours playing jazz and classical records on a hi-fi set. Mark would often stay after school to listen to these records, and at supper-time he would go on and on and on about how great Miles Davis was. Miles was his first musical hero, followed by John Coltrane and Sonny Rollins. Thus he began with highly complex music (before the age of rock) and in later years traveled backward to the early blues and folk songs. In later years, too, he said he was Mick Jagger of The Rolling Stones, and believed what he said. But he never abandoned Miles Davis. Nor did he ever abandon Segovia.

Mark came down with a case of puppy love while he was in Japan. Our housemaid, who cost us $40 a month plus room and board and never stopped working, was no taller than Mark and just as thin. She spoke English with a Southern accent—"purty" was one of her favorite words—and Mark teased her incessantly. Every night after supper when Shigeko was washing dishes, Mark joined her in the kitchen to ask her foolish questions, to tickle her, to muss her hair. Shigeko was very fond of him, and patient, but he didn't know when to stop; and finally she would cry out, "*Mark*, please Mark, no moah, no moah. Mark, you bad." For a month or so Mark practiced pole-vaulting on our lawn and he prevailed upon Shigeko to try it. One of the most mysterious and exotic sights in the Far East was Shigeko running, screaming with laughter, hanging on to the end of a bamboo pole, leaping and then falling to the ground with her legs tucked under her. Always polite, Shigeko landed on her knees.

Mark and I got along all right in Japan, mostly leaving each other alone. I can recall only one unpleasant incident: when we sat down at the supper table, I often reminded Mark to put his napkin in his lap. The more he forgot to do it, the more I nagged him; it was a contest of wills. One evening in the spring I came to the table after my usual brace of strong martinis, and Mark reached for his fork.

"Damn it, Mark, use your napkin!"

He looked a little startled—my voice had a rough edge to it—and he was slow to move.

"All right, goddammit, *don't* use your napkin. If you want to be a boor when you eat, it's all right with me. You'll grow up to be a boor, but *that's* all right. I won't ask you again, ever. I just don't give a damn any more."

Mark put his napkin in his lap. The family meal was eaten in a taut and miserable silence, and at the end of it Mark, crying, jumped up and ran out of the house. I chased him, shouting, "Mark, Mark, you come back here." But I couldn't find him, and I grew more and more angry as I stumbled around in the unpaved, unlit streets. I'd show the little bastard. When I returned home, Mark was already there (he could maneuver through the back alleys very well) and I bawled him out. He sat sullenly on his bed and took it. But I never again reminded him to use his napkin at the dining table. It was absurd, but I wasn't going to stoop to his level.

We flew to San Francisco, my *Stars and Stripes* job finished, on August 5, 1963. It was Mark's fourteenth birthday—the family always seemed to be traveling on his birthday. I was loathe to leave Japan, and so, I think, was Mark. But O'Hara was eager to see Sausalito again, and Pennell could hardly wait. On a hot, airless night a few weeks before we departed, she had said, "Let's get the hell out of this damn country."

In September Mark was enrolled as a freshman at Tamalpais High School in Mill Valley. If I could do it all over again, he never would have set foot in the place.

Mark's dislike of Tam High was immediate. He had come from a school that was loose, libertarian, and experimental. He was forced into a school that was very large, impersonal, and rigid in its concepts of education, notwithstanding its reputation as one of the better high schools in the Bay Area. In his classes Mark really did try, at first; but the style of his attempts had been formed at the American School in Japan, and all he got from the majority of his teachers at Tam was disinterest and discouragement. He submitted to his English teacher a free-verse poem on which he had labored long; it was criticized because it didn't rhyme. He read Kierkegaard's *Concept of Dread* and wrote an essay that was regarded as an esoteric puzzle. Perhaps it was, but an esoteric puzzle, when it comes from a fourteen-year-old boy, should not be ignored. By the end of his freshman year, Mark was coasting.

Not that I was any better than his teacher. Again, as in the past, I paid only scant attention to Mark's schoolwork. But now I had a new excuse for not doing so. Two months before we left Japan I had met and fallen in love with a woman named Mihoko Hirabayashi. She was a dress designer, forty years old, who had never married. Her English was very limited. She was a lovely, gentle person who could give of herself totally, overwhelmingly, both her mind and her body. In Tokyo we had begun an affair. Now, in Sausalito, she occupied my waking thoughts. I wrote long, rambling letters to her from the *Chronicle* office, letters she read with the help of a dictionary. I got drunk and cried to myself because she was so far away. At the same time, I did not want to leave O'Hara. I wanted both women, both lives. Early in 1964 I took advantage of O'Hara's absence—she was in Los Angeles on a visit—to go to Tokyo on a military plane. I told O'Hara that a "junket," a free ride, had been unexpectedly offered me, but actually I was taking a "space available" flight that had required elaborate planning to set up. I stayed a week in Mihoko's apartment. It was a desperate, nightmarish trip; the two of us spent our seven days together being unhappy.

O'Hara, meanwhile, had been asked to run for the Sausalito City Council. She accepted (I could hardly blame her for seeking a diversion outside the home, and she was genuinely concerned about Sausalito's civic future) and she was elected in April. It was a demanding job, without pay, and she devoted hours to it every day.

All this set the atmosphere at home while Mark was a freshman at Tamalpais High School. No wonder that he too sought another world. The civil rights movement was taking shape in the Bay Area, and Mark became active. Regularly, he picketed the Bank of America building in Sausalito after school. He joined San Francisco's "Auto Row" demonstrations to force the hiring of more minority people. He visited friends who lived in Marin City, a black community on the outskirts of Sausalito; and they occasionally came to our house for supper. Once, when I said I was going to walk in a civil rights march across the Golden Gate Bridge to the Federal Building in San Francisco, Mark, aware of my artificial leg, was solicitous in an adult, professional way. "You'll never make it," he said to me. "It's too far. Why don't you drive across the bridge and pick up the march on Lombard Street?" I accepted his advice. And he was right: I never would have made it.

About three o'clock one June morning in 1964, O'Hara was wide awake when I returned home from an unrewarding shift on the *Chronicle* copy desk and several quick drinks at Hanno's, the place where *Chronicle* men drank. I could sense her wakefulness as soon as I opened the bedroom door. Usually I undressed slowly to avoid rousing her (and inviting questions), but now I didn't bother. I took off my clothes and slid into bed. I waited.

"I have something terribly important to tell you,"

O'Hara said. She spoke with a formal clarity, pronouncing all the syllables fully, as she always did when she had something "terribly important" to tell me.

"OK. What is it?"

"Mark has been smoking marijuana."

Maybe O'Hara expected me to sit up in bed and shout, "Oh my God, oh Jesus!" Or go upstairs and challenge Mark to explain his awful deed. After all, it was only 1964. But all I did was say "He has? How do you know?"

"He told me."

"How'd he happen to do that?" With the alcohol in me, I was finding it hard to stay awake.

"He is scared, Bill. He has had a scare. He was doing some homework and all of a sudden he came downstairs and said he wanted to talk to me, alone, without Pennell around, and we went into the bedroom and sat down. Mark said he thought something was the matter with his heart, and that it was going all fluttery now and then. He said some friends of his told him that was what happened when you smoked marijuana. And that he had been smoking it."

"Well, I don't think there's anything wrong with his heart," I said. "But why don't I make an appointment with Dr. Haskell and take him in for a checkup?"

"But the marijuana, Bill. It's dangerous, it's very harmful. And it's illegal. They say you can get all sorts of strange reactions from it. We've got to make him stop it. I think we ought to crack down right away."

"Did he say how he got it?"

"Friends at school. But he would not say which ones."

"For how long?"

"A few months."

"Well, it's not the worst thing in the world. I'll try to take him to the doctor tomorrow." And with that I went to sleep.

Thus it began, in the Chapin family, at 16 Cazneau Avenue, Sausalito, on a day in June.

Chapter 5

THE NEXT DAY I made an appointment with Dr. Robert Haskell, our family physician. Waiting in the car for Mark at Tamalpais High School, I said to myself, "O'Hara's being an alarmist, but I might as well indulge her, it's the easiest way." And when Mark walked down the school steps he did not, in truth, look like your typical dope fiend: he was carrying a load of books, he was neatly dressed in jeans and a checkered sport shirt, his color was healthy, and his hair was combed. He did, however, look somewhat subdued, and he got into the car without saying a word.

Driving toward Sausalito, I questioned him in a calm, detached manner. I asked him how long he had been smoking marijuana. A couple of months. Where did he get it? From friends. What friends? Just friends. What about his heart? Well, it jumped now and then, and that was scary.

I told him I didn't know very much about marijuana,

but that I doubted its ability to damage a heart; and I suggested that the real danger lay in the possibility of arrest. "You could end up in Juvenile Hall." This was my first use of that particular bugaboo; it was not to be my last. Mark did not comment.

When we got to the doctor's office I told Mark to go in by himself while I waited in the car. He returned in an hour. They had taken an electrocardiogram, he said, and his heart was all right. Dr. Haskell phoned me later to say that the pulse was erratic, though not drastically so; and he attributed this to the use of marijuana. The tone of his voice indicated that he was not overly worried about the state of Mark's health.

I had no idea whether marijuana could affect the pulse; I had no ideas about marijuana whatsoever. Years before, a *Chronicle* friend had said he once smoked a marijuana cigarette at a party and later felt as if he were floating while walking down the street. That was the extent of my knowledge.

The summer of 1964, then, was to be a time of learning, because Mark's visit to the doctor did absolutely nothing to dissuade him from the use of marijuana, and marijuana became a presence in our home.

O'Hara and I both learned, but in the process O'Hara was always more aware, more apprehensive. She felt she was fighting something that was extremely difficult to stop, and she was frightened by my casual approach. She wanted me committed to her side as a fellow fighter, and I was not committed. On the contrary, I suspected that O'Hara's crusade against marijuana did more harm than good.

There were discussions with Pennell and Mark—discussions they were careful to keep on an abstract level. (Pennell sided with Mark, but in a more diffident manner; we were fairly sure she smoked marijuana too, but somehow we never thought it would get to be a "problem" for her and it never did.)

We picked up the vocabulary: pot, grass, weed, joints, roaches, lids, getting high, getting stoned. Now, of course, these are common words in lower-, middle-, and upper-class homes. In 1964 they were new; at least they were new to O'Hara and me.

The children said that quite a few kids smoked grass at Tam High. They said it wasn't bad for you, they *knew* that. They cited the La Guardia Report, a 1944 study which said that marijuana had few if any harmful effects and did not lead to antisocial behavior. The La Guardia Report was their bible, their defense manual.

"But it's illegal," we said, the same words that were being said by thousands and thousands of parents to their children.

"So was liquor during prohibition," they said, the same words that were being said by thousands and thousands of children to their parents.

"But that doesn't make it any less dangerous if you get caught with marijuana."

"Well, we don't have any, and besides, people don't very often get caught."

There began to appear the first, contradictory articles in newspapers and magazines. We read them and were confused. Timothy Leary broke into print; the children said, "Listen to Timothy Leary—he's a Harvard psychologist." There were panel debates, lectures, seminars. O'Hara and I attended many of them. At Tamalpais High School Matthew O'Connor, a top official with the State Bureau of Narcotic Enforcement, told an attentive audience of parents and students that his agents risked their lives in wild battles with crazed marijuana users. The students groaned in disbelief; most of the parents nodded their heads. At Sausalito's Episcopal Church, the late James Pike, Bishop of the California Diocese, waved a copy of the La Guardia Report (admitting that he hadn't read it) and denounced our hypocritical attitude toward marijuana. I had been irritated by O'Connor's point of view, and now I was just as irritated by Bishop Pike's manner. I tended to agree with his permissive approach; but he tried to be so much "with it," a hippie in a clergyman's collar, and I thought he seemed phony. And if he was going to cite the La Guardia Report at least he could have read it.

All the while Mark was smoking grass almost every day. O'Hara was acutely conscious of this; I was not. Frequently when I arrived home early in the morning after work, she would be lying in bed wide awake, as she had been on that day in June, the day she first told me about Mark and marijuana.

"Bill?"

"Yeah. What is it?"

"Mark was high again today, I'm sure of it. He didn't get home for supper until seven."

"How do you know he was high?"

"Well, the way he acted. His eyes were reddish. Besides, I can smell it when he's been smoking. I can smell it on him."

"O'Hara, you can't *smell* it unless he's actually smoking."

"Yes I can. I *know* I can."

"OK, OK, OK. So you can."

"Bill, you don't seem to care. We've *got* to stop him."

"How?"

"I don't know. But we've got to think of something. Maybe we ought to move to another part of the country."

"That wouldn't do any good. If he really wants it, he can get it anywhere."

"I know, but not as much as around here. Tam High's full of it."

"Well, so long as he doesn't get busted I don't think it does him much harm. It's a pretty mild drug, you know."

And I would drift off to sleep, snoring, with O'Hara still awake, angry, frustrated—and alone.

She repeatedly put up warning signals in the vain hope that I would heed them. When Mark was out of the house O'Hara would find a roach in an ashtray while cleaning his room—and show it to me. Or she would find a package of Zig-Zag cigarette paper—and show it to me. I shrugged them off. So what? O'Hara was being hysterical and her methods smacked of the police. You couldn't force a teen-ager to do anything; the answer was persuasion and patience. And as for moving to another part of the country, that was absurd. I was content to stay in Sausalito; I liked the town (and it was as close as I could get to Tokyo).

Did Mark also put up warning signals during this initial phase of using drugs? Yes, he did, but I refused to accept them as such. When I asked him point-blank if he was smoking marijuana, he always denied it. This was preposterous, since the evidence was in plain sight: the roaches, the little plastic bags in the corners of his bedroom closet, the corncob pipes. His carelessness must have been deliberate. And his habits were revealing: every day during summer vacation he slept late, until ten or eleven; he was drowsy in the morning; at noon he would say, "Can I go downtown? Can I go downtown to the Tides and read some books?"

It was O'Hara who usually answered. "OK, but let's settle on a time. Four o'clock. You be home by four o'clock so I can give you supper the same time I feed Dad before he goes to work."

Sometimes, rarely, he would be home by four o'clock —and stoned, although I didn't realize it then. He would drag into the house, his eyes red, his face remote, and put on a phonograph record—Coltrane, Thelonious Monk, Miles Davis—and lie on the living room sofa half-asleep until O'Hara called him to the table. He was in a distant realm.

It was more the rule however, for him to stay out until six or seven or eight or nine or ten o'clock at night. And invariably his absence meant a series of useless phone calls, as O'Hara went down her list of phone numbers of his friends in Sausalito and Mill Valley.

"Hello, is Mark there?"

"Aah—no."

"Do you know where he is?"

"No."

"OK, thank you. If you happen to see him, tell him to phone home, will you?"

On weekends I made these calls. Mark was never there. I wonder how often he really *was* there, next to the phone, listening to these futile exchanges of non-information. And I wonder, too, why I didn't punish him —by taking away privileges—when he stayed out late and his supper got cold. It's possible he would have welcomed it, clung to it like an anchor in the sea.

It is remarkable how stubborn Mark could be in his denials, even when I shoved the stuff right under his nose. One day, while working in the back yard. I spotted a jelly jar underneath the sundeck, half-concealed by a wooden support. In the jar was a plastic bag and in the bag was a wad of greenish-brown, fragmented leaves. I assumed they were marijuana, naturally—and a good-sized "stash" at that. I showed my find to Mark. He turned away from me, saying he had no idea where it came from; and then when I started toward the toilet, to flush it down, he said it was oregano he was planning to use in an "experiment" and he wanted to keep it. I flushed it down anyway (the customary way to get rid of marijuana in our house) and he must have been very angry at the waste, though he didn't show it.

On another day I happened to glance up at a level section of our roof—a place that Mark could reach through his bedroom window. Near the rain gutter, out in the open, was a flat wooden box with a few bedraggled plants sprouting from it. I said, "Holy Jesus," asked myself if the neighbors had seen it, and ran upstairs. The plants were marijuana, but the soil was soggy, and it was apparent that Mark's attempt to grow his own was a failure. Again he denied everything; but Pennell was listening; she gave him a long look and laughed.

I'm sure that Mark, as he descended further and further into drugs, confided in Pennell, and she also put up a warning signal. She got drunk at a dance by joining with her date in the consumption of a pint of gin in the back seat of a car, fell down, hit her head on the curb, cracked a tooth, and had to be taken, semi-comatose, to Marin General Hospital. When I arrived she was on an examination table, a doctor standing over her. She smelled of gin. She sobbed uncontrollably, overcome by grief and shame. I put my head down near hers and tried to comfort her. She put her arms around my neck and cried out, "Help me, help me. Oh please help me. My brother's hooked on drugs."

Pennell had to get drunk before she could betray her younger brother.

Gradually, as the summer ran its course, suspicions grew and faith disappeared. Of the many changes in the Chapin family that drugs effected this was the most damaging: the loss of trust. It will always be partly gone, even if Mark has a complete recovery. Faith will never have a complete recovery.

O'Hara and I became spies in our own house—cops, detectives, informers, agents. We became mean-minded allies—against Mark. Whenever he said, "Can I go downtown?" and got permission and left the house, one of his parents would climb the stairs to his room as if drawn by a magnet. We searched his clothes, turned his pockets inside out, probed the cuffs of his trousers. We looked behind the books in his bookcase, slid our hands beneath his mattress, ransacked his desk. We *wanted* to find marijuana, we *wanted* the small taste of horror that accompanied the finding of a hidden joint. "Ha! I've got you, Mark. You can't fool me. I've got the goods on you this time!"

But if there was a cheap, melodramatic thrill in this business of being a spy there was also shame, and on occasion there was humiliation.

One warm and windless Saturday night I received a call from a distraught mother who said that her daughter Lisa had been with Mark earlier in the day, had failed to come home, it was past ten o'clock, and did I know where they might be? No, I did not, but I could guess they might be aboard the *Charles Van Damme* and I would try to find them.

The *Charles Van Damme* was an old broken-down ferryboat that had once plied the bay. Now, permanently lodged in the mud flats at the northern end of Sausalito, it was a teen-age club. Rock groups played, kids danced, soft drinks were sold, and pot was smoked. Pennell and Mark were steady customers of the *Van Damme*. It was a place where kids could go without being hassled by their parents.

By going to the *Van Damme* to hassle a kid, I was violating a taboo. The minute I walked up the rickety gangplank I felt like an alien, an unwanted stranger. I felt watched and I *was* watched. I wandered here and there in the dim light, with the rock music thudding in my ears and the smoke burning in my eyes. I saw boys and girls I knew, and I asked them if they had seen Mark or Lisa. No, not tonight. None of them had seen Mark or Lisa, they said, and I was sure they were lying. Sitting at tables around the dance floor, they stared at me as I walked past seeking my son. Their stares seemed to ask if I really believed they would fink on him. Finally I went home, and Mark got in about midnight. He said he had been at a friend's house in Mill Valley playing records. Later, much later, I learned that Mark, aboard the *Van Damme*, had been warned of my approach before I even set foot on the boat. The warning system was swift and efficient. He and Lisa hid under a table. Every person I talked to must have been aware of what was going on, and must have been pleased by it.

That's what it was like to be a cop, on the prowl, out to bust my own son.

On another night, while I was shaking down Mark's room, I poked into a Mexican leather satchel hanging from his closet door. This was a place you would put something if you wanted it discovered, and what I discovered was a plastic cylinder of pills and capsules, perhaps forty of them, in great variety: reds, yellows, greens, round ones, flat ones, long ones. I was jolted. Marijuana? Of course. But what was he doing with this junk?

As soon as he got home I walked upstairs with him, closed his bedroom door, and showed him the pills.

"Where'd you get these, Mark?"

"I dunno."

"Come on, you'd better tell me."

"From Greg." Greg was a schoolmate; his father was a pharmacist.

"Have you taken any of them?"

"No, I was just holding them for Greg."

"What the hell do you mean, *holding* them?"

"You know, just holding them."

"Does Greg use them?"

"I dunno."

"Bullshit, Mark. Come on, tell the truth."

He sat on the bed, huddled up, avoiding my eyes. He wouldn't answer.

"Come on, Mark. For Christ's sake, open up."

Silence.

"Mark, you don't even know what these pills *are,* I'll bet. You don't even know what they might *do* to you."

Silence.

Suddenly I sat next to him and put my arm around his shoulders, held him tight, and began to cry. "Mark, what's going to happen to you? How can we help you? What can we do for you?"

This burst of emotion must have astonished him, it was so abrupt, so unexpected.

He didn't respond to it; he tried to pull away. He was embarrassed; his instinct was to get away from this scene. And he was silent. Though he could still send out a warning signal, he could not follow through on it.

I left him. For the first time I had concrete proof that Mark was fooling around with more than marijuana, and for the first time I was frightened. O'Hara, of course, thought I should have been frightened months ago. And so had Pennell when she got drunk. Their warnings were in vain.

Chapter 6

DURING THAT SUMMER of 1964 Mark took his first LSD trip. The result, or what O'Hara and I saw of the result, was alarming, but it hardly seemed catastrophic.

Mark took the trip in the company of a dozen friends, and their leader, the "guru" who proposed to illuminate their minds.

I did not know the "guru" well. He was a pleasant boy, quiet, gentle, handsome, and three years older than Mark. The two of them, according to Mark, talked about freedom of education and Oriental mysticism. His father was a plumber, his mother a city planner, and he himself was a genius. Bored by teachers who couldn't teach him, he had dropped out of high school, though later he went to college. It was said that he had taken a Scholastic Achievement Test and got the top score of 800.

On a Saturday morning in July the guru and his friends—Pennell and Mark among them—hitchhiked to Stinson Beach, a West Marin town where campers, hippies, and tourists shared the sand and the sea. The group gathered at a spot that was mostly dunes and tall grass, away from outsiders, and the guru told them (we were to learn) that under his guidance they would have a pleasurable and instructive trip. The atmosphere was right: blue sky, sun, waves, open beach, peace and quiet. Relax, there was nothing to fear, he said, and they all took lysergic acid diethylamide. How large the dosage was I'll never know, though the leader probably did know, because he was neither stupid nor careless. He was merely, in my view, afflicted with the insanity of total brilliance.

At seven o'clock that night Pennell and Mark were not home, and though this was not unusual for Mark, it was for Pennell, so we began to fret and to use the telephone. We found no sign of them. About ten o'clock, they walked in the front door and went directly to their rooms, without stopping to check the refrigerator for food, without more than the briefest greeting.

"Where've you been?"

"Nowhere."

It was quiet upstairs. Both children got straight into bed, which was not like them. Then Pennell began to cry, and O'Hara and I went up. She cried in a fussy, spasmodic way, softly, and she couldn't say why she was crying. She could say, however, that she and Mark had taken LSD. It was impossible to get details.

"What was it like, Pennell?"

"I don't know."

"What happened?"

"I don't know. I felt funny."

"What was it like, Mark?"

"I saw blue lights."

"Were you scared?"

"Yes, I was scared."

They both had difficulty getting to sleep, but the next day they seemed perfectly normal. They did not seem metamorphosed in any way. They were reluctant to talk about their experience at Stinson Beach.

This was at a time when LSD was no more than a worrisome shadow on the horizon of American consciousness. There were reports, not widely circulated, that it was being tested as a drug for schizophrenics. Timothy Leary, a man whom I would be inclined to attack physically if I ever met him, was preaching that LSD would help people "know themselves." The word "psychedelic" was new. I myself had barely heard of LSD. But one story, related to me by a *Chronicle* copy boy, had stuck in my mind. A friend of his, he said, had taken LSD at a party, walked out of a third-floor window, and fallen to his death.

The day after Mark's trip I went to the guru's home in Mill Valley and met his parents. Neither he nor his younger brother were there. His parents, like their sons, were quiet, self-possessed people. It was a serene home, I felt, a home where love prevailed. And as a casual guest in that home, I was puzzled: why did this boy need something else, why did he need LSD?

Sitting at the kitchen table drinking coffee, I gave the parents a sketchy account of the Stinson Beach trip. Their reaction was mild; it was nothing to get excited about, it didn't even seem to surprise them. The father said that his son was a mature, responsible boy who was capable of making his own decisions. He implied that it was up to him to take LSD or not to take it. They had discussed it, yes, on an intellectual level, and he had got from his son a promise that he would never give the drug to anyone else. Listening to these calm, measured words, I felt like screaming, "Jesus Christ, the world's on fire and you just sit there," but all I said was, "Apparently your son broke his promise."

"Well, we don't really know that for a certainty, do we? I'll talk to him when he gets home."

He suggested, quite logically, that I learn more about LSD, and before I said goodby he gave me a copy of an article describing the LSD experiments of a Dr. Abram Hoffer in Saskatchewan, Canada. He said it was very interesting, and asked if he could please have it back when I was finished.

I read the article. Dr. Hoffer was using LSD in the treatment of alcoholics. By inducing "good" hallucinations he hoped to wean them away from their addiction to alcohol. The article emphasized that LSD should not be taken except under controlled conditions, with a doctor in attendance. It said that LSD dosages had to be progressively increased to bring on hallucinations; there was an immunity factor. It described some of the patients' visions: legs and arms that disattached themselves and floated in space; clocks that started to walk, walls that moved, sounds that invaded the brain, colors that swirled overhead.

A visual, aural, and tactile nightmare. I couldn't understand why a person would voluntarily swallow LSD.

I showed the article to Pennell and Mark. I told them about the boy who had fallen from the window. I said I thought LSD was incredibly dangerous. Pennell said she would never take it again. Mark said he would never take it again. Two weeks later Mark took it again, and this time his trip made the Stinson Beach trip seem like a morning in kindergarten.

It began on a Friday afternoon, so far as I can reconstruct it, and it lasted all weekend. Mark and a friend had gone downtown; it is probable they went there to purchase, or to be given, sugar cubes soaked in LSD. I saw them walking back up the hill—tall, slender, one with red hair, the other blond. They shared an interest in poetry, music, and drugs. Mark, as they approached, noticed me standing in the doorway and he shouted that he was going to his friend's house. I said sure, that was OK, not to be late for supper.

He didn't come home that night, and the next morning I called his friend's home. No one I talked to knew where either of the boys were, and I had a premonition. I was certain that bad trouble was ahead, the worst yet.

O'Hara and I set a new record for telephone calls,

calling home after home, and all the while our anxiety increased. Often we talked to adolescents, and I had a terrible sense that these young people were trying to conceal Mark, to protect him from me. I had a terrible sense that they knew Mark was on a trip beyond anything I could understand and that they had to keep him away from me until he had returned to my world. I felt confusion and conspiracy all around me. Sometimes a young voice would answer my call and when I said, "Is Mark there?" the owner of the young voice would simply hang up.

He didn't come home Saturday night either. We called the police stations of several Marin County communities. The officers said they had no reports of a Mark Chapin. Late Sunday afternoon Mark Chapin walked into the house. He was alone.

We both jumped on him. "Where the hell have you been? Why didn't you at least let us know where you were?" He stared with eyes that wouldn't recognize us, and then abruptly went upstairs and got on the phone. I could hear scraps of the conversation—something about music, something about a band, something about his mother and father. Then he appeared again, just as abruptly, and said, "I gotta go out."

"No, Mark, no! You stay here. We want to talk to you."

"Can't. I gotta go."

He ran out of the house and down the driveway into the street, with me after him, shouting. He looked back at me, over his shoulder, and ran even faster. I couldn't possibly keep up with him. With his LSD vision, I may have been a monster, a huge, vengeful monster hunting him.

Two blocks away from the house Mark turned a corner and disappeared from view. I got in my car and followed. I saw him once, a quick glimpse. He was still running and still looking back, and when he saw me in the car he ducked behind a garage. I cruised the streets slowly, like a cop in a patrol car, lacking only the revolving red light, after my own son. But I wasn't sure whether I wanted to punish him or save him. It began to get dark. Acting on a hunch, I drove north on Highway 101 and turned into the lateral road leading to Mill Valley. There, on the sidewalk next to a row of tract houses, I saw Mark again. He was half-running, slower now; he stumbled, caught himself, and moved on. He seemed exhausted and in full panic as the "other" world closed in on him. As I drew near, he spotted me and lunged up a side street into the housing tract. I followed. But I lost him in the darkness, and after driving aimlessly through the tract for fifteen minutes, I returned home. There was nothing to do but wait.

O'Hara and I waited. It was not unlikely that he would stay overnight at another house, but we waited for him, and a few minutes before midnight he came in the door.

This was a different Mark. He was quiet, slow, played out and sad. And he was peaceful in a strange way, as if the terror and the torment had been drained from him. He sat with us, and we gently questioned him. I asked if he had taken LSD and he said yes he had, he had taken it last Friday and it was like a million orchestras exploding in his head. Why had he bolted out of the house? He didn't know. What had he done? He had roamed the streets of Mill Valley. He had thought about God. God, as he walked, kept entering his consciousness. And with God present he had wandered into a church—he thought it was the Christian Science Church but he wasn't sure— and he had been welcomed by "a nice man." Together they had discussed God.

Before Mark went to bed I talked to him again about LSD. Why had he taken it? He said he didn't know.

And it is impossible even now, years later, to say exactly why Mark took LSD, or to estimate how many times he took it. His own accounts vary wildly, depending on the emotions and needs of the moment. Does he want to impress me with how desperate he has been, how reckless? Does he want to be a martyr? He will tell me he has dropped acid more than a hundred times. Does he

want to impress me with how responsible he has been,
what a good boy he is? He will tell me he has taken no
more than ten acid trips, and always someone else forced
the stuff on him. He will even stare straight at me and say
he has never taken LSD, it was all a made-up story, an
adolescent dream.

Who knows? This is a swamp, a wilderness.

When Mark woke up after his visit with the "nice
man," he was still thinking church. I said church was
fine if that was what he wanted, and I would be willing
to help him. O'Hara and I were atheists, and Mark was
aware of this. Not once had we ever taken him to church.
To me church was rubbish, and the Christian Science
Church was the worst kind of rubbish. But Mark, searching for *any* resolution of his doubts and fears, unable to
find it within his own mind and getting scant support
from his father, was groping feebly for "a church." He
visited the Reading Room of the Christian Science Church
in Sausalito (it was only a couple of blocks away) and
brought home a thick pile of booklets. the life of Mary
Baker Eddy, *Faith and Healing*, the whole business. He
opened a few of the booklets; most of them remained on
his desk untouched. They bored him. He asked me if I
would talk to the nice man, and I said sure. He was the
Mill Valley minister. He said he would be ever so happy
to see Mark on a regular basis and to guide him into the
Church of Christ, Scientist. I urged Mark to accept
the offer, but faced with that bit of reality he drew back,
and after two weeks Christian Science was a dead issue.

Then O'Hara and I turned Mark toward psychiatry
and pushed him into the therapist's office. This was the
wrong way to do it, woefully wrong. If I had said to
Mark, "Look, I think you've got serious emotional problems, and I think your use of drugs is dangerous; but
under *no* circumstances should you consider going to a
psychiatrist, you've got to work it out yourself," then possibly Mark would have replied, in time, "I'd like to see a

psychiatrist." Instead, O'Hara and I pushed him, while he dug in his heels.

And our method of choosing a psychiatrist was no method at all; it was as foolish as closing our eyes and stabbing a finger into the medical section of the telephone book yellow pages. Our own therapeutic experience and countless warnings from professional friends should have taught us that one decides on a psychiatrist after the most careful research. But O'Hara and I were distracted; anxiety ruled us.

The doctor we chose was a tall, angular man with a perpetual look of owlish wisdom. Later on I began calling him "The Owl," though not to his face. The only reason we chose him was that Pennell had asked for some psychotherapy a year before and had chosen him, and the only reason Pennell had chosen him was that one of her girl friends had gone to him. Pennell had commented vaguely, "He sort of helped me, I guess," but had said little more than that; and I knew nothing from anyone else of The Owl's education, personal background, psychiatric approach, or reputation. I had seen him when he opened the door to usher Pennell into his inner office. I had seen him peer through his heavy black horn-rimmed glasses and nod gently to my daughter. That was all.

But we chose this therapist for Mark; and Mark, angry and silent, was hauled off to see him once a week. He hated it. He didn't put it into words, but he had no respect for this man, and he missed several sessions, simply by failing to show up for his drive to the therapist's office; so we arranged the appointments at a time when we could intercept Mark as he emerged from school.

The Owl was not one to be generous with information, but he did tell me once that it was very difficult to persuade Mark to talk during therapy sessions. I was eventually to learn, however, that this $25-an-hour therapist thought his role was to serve as a receptacle, a sort of well for information, so that he actually tried very little persuasion. It was up to the patient to communicate with him and thereby achieve catharsis. The Owl, for the most part, just sat motionless in his modern leather-padded chair and waited. But Mark didn't talk.

While these silent (and surely excruciating) sessions were proceeding, Mark returned to Tamalpais High School as a sophomore, and was dealt a bitter blow. He applied for admission to a special humanities course that ordinarily was limited to juniors and seniors. It was a good course, popular with students, with a great deal of freedom and a lot of "adult" reading; and Mark must have sensed that he would need more of a challenge than he would get from the standard sophomore curriculum. Besides, as a freshman he had earned excellent grades: four A's and a B plus.

His counselor turned him down. We intervened; we said Mark was bright enough and creative enough to be accepted, and furthermore, Martha Wax, one of Mark's closest friends, had been accepted as a sophomore. But it was no use; Mark was excluded.

He already felt that formal education was suspect, despite his good year in Tokyo; now he was convinced that it was worthless, a bummer, and his grades began their long, uninterrupted slide into the pit.

Drugs, more than ever, absorbed his life.

Chapter 7

IGHTS, QUARRELS, RECRIMINATIONS, and resentments prevailed in the Chapin household through the fall, winter, and spring of 1964–1965, and most of the trouble centered on Mark. One day he would be the victim, the next day the catalyst.

There were fights over drugs, little different from those I have already described, but more frequent.

There were fights over Mark's refusal to do any homework. "Mark, for God's sake, do some studying. You'll never get into college."

"I don't want to get into college. What does it matter?"

And there were fights (the great cliché of the generation gap) over the length of Mark's hair. These were the most senseless fights of all.

In the Battle of Hair, Mark and O'Hara were the opponents and I was the compromiser. O'Hara's view, she claimed, was pragmatic: if Mark's hair was reasonably short the police would be less inclined to pick him up for questioning, or for whatever; and O'Hara lived in constant fear that Mark would be picked up with marijuana in his pocket. For Mark, of course, here was a challenge; he was damned if his parents were going to dictate so many inches above the neckline. And I, truly, did not feel that hair should become a family issue. I suggested to O'Hara that Mark's fierce determination to keep the hair on his head might be sexually motivated—he didn't want his balls cut off—and O'Hara suggested that I was being much too theoretical. As Mark's hair grew, so did O'Hara's anxiety. Mark helped not at all by refusing to comb it; his hair became a wild red mop, the symbol of his rebellion. O'Hara dreaded the moment when Mark, sleepy-eyed, would clump downstairs in the morning. All she could see was his hair. All she could talk about, it often seemed to me, was his hair.

Getting Mark to go to the barber meant an all-day struggle: screams, threats, counterthreats, offers of rewards, wheedlings, and much profanity. O'Hara would promise Mark that Sandy the Barber would not cut it too short; he'd just trim it. Strict instructions would be issued to Sandy the Barber. One day Mark returned home with what looked distressingly like a crewcut—it was almost as short as my hair. Sandy had been absent-minded or mean or both. Mark was livid. He ran upstairs, cursing O'Hara and fighting back tears. I shouted up to him that he'd have to apologize to O'Hara for his language. *"Fuck you!"* he shouted back. I hurried up to his room and we glared at each other, silently, breathing hard. It would have been funny if it hadn't been sad.

After that, Mark stopped going to the barber. O'Hara cut his hair, but it was never really short. And Mark began to save the precious locks that fell from O'Hara's scissors to the sundeck. There is a plastic bag in Mark's desk that contains hair. It resides in the desk drawer with page after page of crazy poetry and pencils and dark glasses and stones from the beach.

There were fights, too, over Mark's choice of com-

panions. O'Hara and I wanted him to have wholesome
friends who were molded in the image of his parents;
Mark wanted friends who had cast off the tiresome rules
of middle-class convention, friends who were rebels.

One of these fights ended violently. Mark had come
home, late as usual, with a boy whose reputation was not
reassuring. He was said to be the brilliant son of a concert
pianist, who had whipped him cruelly; he was a sports-car
driver who apparently got a morbid thrill by risking his
and his passengers' lives; and he was far gone, much of
the time, on drugs. Pennell told us he'd had countless acid
trips. I saw this boy once at the Sausalito Arts Festival,
where it was not difficult to be accepted as an exhibitor.
He was kneeling on the ground, babbling, glassy-eyed,
and trying ever so slowly to put incoherent watercolors on
a sheet of paper. I felt pity and horror as I watched him;
now, when he was in my house, I felt anxiety.

The boy was wearing make-up, a smear of rouge on
his cheeks and lipstick on his mouth, and his clothes were
strangely theatrical. An actor in a masque. He was quiet,
but he had an ominous air; and I thought, "The make-up
isn't because he's queer, it's because he's an acid head."
He and Mark went into the television room, sat on a
couch, and talked. I could only hear blurred phrases and
an occasional laugh, but I was suspicious of them. Every
fifteen minutes or so Mark came into the living room and
asked if he could go downtown again with his friend.
I said no he couldn't, he had been late for supper as it
was. I wanted them apart. He persisted, and finally I
yelled at him, "No! You can't!"

"Why?"

"Because I say so, that's why."

"You're dead."

As Mark spoke, he turned and moved quickly toward
the television room. He must have sensed that in declar-
ing me dead he would get a strong response. And he did.

"Don't touch me," he shouted as I reached for him
with both hands, lunging forward. He swung his fists,

but he did not actually make contact, and I didn't swing back at him. We swirled down a corridor into the dining room, with O'Hara and Pennell in pursuit, trying to separate us. Then I caught a vivid glimpse of Pennell sliding down a wall into a heap on the floor, where she burst into tears; and as Mark and I tussled, I thought, "It's not Pennell's fault. It's a shame to get her involved in this mess."

In a few seconds Mark broke free from me and ran to the street. His friend, understandably, had fled. I followed Mark outside, trying to reestablish the "proper" attitude of father toward son and son toward father. I ordered him inside and, in the television room with doors closed, bawled him out for five minutes straight. The burden of it was, "Don't you ever again tell me I'm dead."

That was our first physical fight and my reaction to it was snobbish: in the Chapin family this did not happen, it was too sordid. Later we had other physical fights, and my reaction became less and less snobbish. One learns.

But the differences between Mark and me did not inevitably explode into wrestling matches or even into shouting matches. Indeed, my propriety still saw to it that usually we expressed our differences in more subtle fashion. Take, for example, the time Mark wrote a poem about contemporary death, a poem that I (knowing very little about poetry) considered good enough to be published. Mark wrote it in January, 1965, when he was fifteen:

> It took not even a moment.
> He was there in a shot of oil
> Falling from the orange and dying sun,
> As they say.
> KeirUmBoom, he was thinking as
> He opened his eyes
> To the beautiful yellow sphere,
> Its surface a shifting mask
> Which showed no face.
> And being a fool, he thought—
> Well, here it comes.
> A fire is rushing me
> To the void of death

And I must be given time to think.
And so he sat down
To observe this spark
Of future emptiness
And he soon decided
That this flame would die
Long before it could ever come here.
And there he was sitting
With this thought
Which had just oozed
From his huge dark nasal cage,
Or his brain rather.
When, then it came
And he couldn't see it
But he knew it was there.
And then it was dark.

To me the poem was a strong evocation of nuclear terror; I told Mark I thought it was excellent, and I did not patronize him by saying, "for someone your age." He was enormously pleased. "Do you think we ought to send it somewhere?" he asked.

I was really impressed by the poem, but his question put me in a quandary. Where to send it? It was not a children's poem, and to submit it to a children's magazine would be foolish, I felt. To send it to an adults' magazine would risk rejection, and I was fearful of what, at this stage, rejection would do to Mark. So I stalled. But Mark would have none of my stalling, now that the idea of publication had been ignited. Every day he pestered me, and eventually, without saying that it was a poem written by a teen-ager, I sent it to *Prairie Schooner*, published at the University of Nebraska. The reason for choosing *Prairie Schooner* escapes me.

Weeks passed, then months, and there was no word from *Prairie Schooner*. Daily Mark asked, "Did you hear anything about the poem, Dad?" I began to think he suspected that I had never sent it; I imagined that he blamed me for the long silence. In April I mailed a follow-up

letter, explaining that I was a father acting on behalf of
his son. On May 10 I got this reply:

Dear Mr. Chapin:
We have read this poem with interest. Although we cannot
use it in *Prairie Schooner,* we do think it shows talent, and
your son should certainly be encouraged to work on. He
has some good images, a general feel for rhythm and drama,
but he needs to work more on total clarity.
                              Best wishes.
                              Bernice Slote,
                              Editor

   Mark had an overweening fear of failure—a perceptive teacher once told me this was central to his problems
—and his reaction to the *Prairie Schooner* incident was far
out of proportion to its importance. He seemed crushed,
silent, and resentful of me. I tried to reassure him. I said
one had to expect a hundred rejection slips before an acceptance, and that this did not mean you were not going
to succeed.
   Never again did he ask me to submit a poem. And I,
in turn, took on a burden of guilt that was pointless. I
assumed that Mark felt I had somehow betrayed him; and
the whole business, with all of its injured feelings, became more damaging than an out-in-the-open fistfight.

   But these were painful days for all of us. A lot of the
pain in 1964–1965 was caused by my absent mind, which
was often 5,000 miles away, in Japan, with Mihoko Hirabayashi. The fantasies of many of my days and nights were
taken up by Mihoko, and when this happened, Mark and
O'Hara were just pieces of furniture in my house. Then
Mihoko came to San Francisco, with disastrous results.
   In October, 1964, I flew to Tokyo to write feature
stories about the Olympic Games for the *Chronicle*—at
least that was my excuse for going—and I stayed three
weeks. I lived with Mihoko in her apartment, which was

built to accommodate dolls, and returned to Sausalito with high blood pressure, which I still have.

Two months later, I asked Mihoko, by mail, to come to San Francisco. She understood me to mean that I wanted her in San Francisco permanently, and her reply sounded ecstatic. I was inviting her just for a visit, but I didn't have the heart or the guts to tell her so. The plan for her to move was rash and preposterous, and I was certain it would fail. One day, before she arrived in January, I wrote her a wretched letter. I said I was sorry, *gomen nasai,* it was hopeless; I loved her, but stay in Tokyo. That night I went to a dinner party where I sat next to an insufferable bore. He talked steadily and his breath was bad. "Christ," I thought, "there is more to life than *this,*" and I drank too much. In the morning I managed to retrieve the letter from a mail carrier before it reached the post office. Mihoko flew to the United States two weeks later. She had a six-months visa; we didn't talk about what would happen after the six months. We did talk about my family, and Mihoko was always solicitous, especially about Mark, whom she had never met. She had, however, met O'Hara—at drinking parties in Tokyo—and I didn't think she even considered herself a rival.

I set up Mihoko in a basement flat near the ocean in San Francisco—a dark, gloomy place but the best we could find, the best I felt I could afford. Mihoko's almost complete lack of English was a heavy handicap, and she led a lonely life. She walked for hours in Golden Gate Park.

Meanwhile, there were developments at the *Chronicle.* My articles on the Olympics had been highly praised, and I, restless and fed up with the copy desk, asked for a writing job. I got more than I had bargained for.

The newspaper's executive editor invited me to write a daily sports column. It was to be witty, offbeat, hypercritical—the successor, actually, to a sports column "invented" by Charles McCabe and later abandoned by him in favor of a column of wider scope. The *Chronicle* had been shopping around for a year for someone who could emulate McCabe in the sports section. I was flattered and excited by the proposal. I was also scared shitless.

To qualify as a columnist, I had to submit a dozen sample columns. If these were approved by the publisher and the executive editor, I would be given a three-months trial; and if the public responded, the column would be actively promoted and I would get a substantial raise. If the public didn't respond, I would go back to the copy desk.

My first task was to compose the samples, while I continued to run the copy desk. The pressures were too great. I was trying to see Mihoko every night after work, and I didn't know what to do with her except go to bed. When I was home I couldn't sleep; I'd lie awake for hours clenching and unclenching my fists as if that would make everything go away. I couldn't write; sitting down at the typewriter was an exercise in terror.

I resolved the situation by collapsing and confessing to O'Hara, a long outburst of anguish and guilt. She might have thrown me out right then, I suppose, or walked out herself. Instead, she listened quietly and then made me a cup of tea. I had been lying on the couch crying convulsively, almost screaming. While the tea was brewing, I got to my feet, and I felt my brain tilt. It was as though all my senses had gone slightly askew; I was afraid that if I took one step forward I would fall. I sat down, and put my head in my arms, and later I drank my cup of tea.

That night, on the premise that I would be better off busy, I went to work, and after work I saw Mihoko. She was as sweet and gentle as ever. At two o'clock in the morning I told her that I had told O'Hara. It came as no surprise to her. She must have known that I was coming apart, and that she would have to return to Tokyo.

In July, 1965, she did return and I have not seen her since, nor do I expect to. In the interim I seldom saw her in San Francisco, though I called her almost every day from my *Chronicle* office. I worried constantly that she might kill herself—once Mihoko had said of her existence in that San Francisco apartment, "I almost die, Beel," and I believed her—and this left me with little capacity to worry about Mark, much less think rationally about him.

My responses to him, during the rare times that we talked, were automatic. I assumed he knew nothing about Mihoko; but he was still perceptive, and my troubled, erratic mind surely puzzled and frightened him. I was an absentee father.

Throughout this turmoil, O'Hara remained strong because somebody had to be strong. I was startled by her outward serenity—she encouraged me to try to write the sample sports columns, she was calm, and she rarely mentioned Mihoko, except once or twice to show that she shared my concern over the possibility of suicide.

O'Hara also arranged for me to see Mark's psychiatrist. "Well, I understand you have some problems yourself," The Owl said to me at the initial session. "Perhaps I can help you. I've taken a special interest in writers. I do some writing myself." It was virtually the longest speech he ever made to me. He wanted to see me three times a week (I wondered, "Does this mean I'm three times as sick as Mark?"), and I agreed. I was ready to agree to anything.

Somehow, the sample columns got written, and the column was launched on April 19, opening day of the Giants' baseball season at Candlestick Park. Column Number One fell short of being a masterpiece, and its impact on sports fans was diminished by a typographical omission that rendered it utterly pointless.

A week after my debut the *Chronicle* sent me to Lewiston, Maine, to cover the Cassius Clay–Sonny Liston heavyweight title fight. It was a rough journey. I swallowed tranquilizers like popcorn, lost my suitcase and found it again, got so tense I broke a blood vessel in one eye, and drank heavily.

On my return to San Francisco I discovered that the publisher of the *Chronicle*, Charles deYoung Thieriot, was irritated by the title of the column, facetiously called "The

Expert." Thieriot ordered it changed to "Chapin's Chowder."

"Jesus Christ," I said to the managing editor when he brought me this dreadful information. "That's not good enough for the *Toonerville Times*."

"I know, I know," said the managing editor, "but Charlie wants it that way. He loves alliteration. He's a strange man, Bill, a strange man."

I didn't put up much of a fight. "Well, it's *his* paper," I said, and went home to drink two giant martinis and complain to O'Hara about "Chapin's Chowder."

We were at the supper table when I made my complaints. Mark listened with rising interest, his attention switching from his food to my angry words, and suddenly he said, "It'll ruin you, you know."

That staggered me. What he really meant, it seemed to me, was: "It'll ruin *me*, Mark; I'll be laughed at in school. Who wants to be known as the son of a guy who writes something called 'Chapin's Chowder'?" For an instant I was struck by how much I had been taking Mark for granted. And then, emboldened by the two giant martinis, I left the table and called the managing editor. I said it was Charlie Thieriot's newspaper but my name, and under no circumstances was the column to appear the next morning under the title "Chapin's Chowder." If Charlie insisted, then kill the column.

The column appeared with no title at all, and it never did get a title during the sixteen months of its existence, although I suggested several alliterative ones. It was identified only by "William Chapin."

That statement of Mark's—"It'll ruin you"—was the most interest he ever showed in the column. Usually he ignored it, or dismissed it with a few words I took to be contemptuous.

I hated him for his contempt.

Chapter 8

*I*T WAS ELEVEN O'CLOCK on a Saturday night, Mark's supper was in a warm oven waiting for him, dried out, and Mark's location was unknown. The routine series of inquiries had failed again, and so had my excursions in the car. O'Hara was reading, and I, pretending to read, was worrying about Mihoko and the sports column soon to be born. The phone rang and I answered.

"Is this Mr. William Chapin?"

"Yes."

"This is the San Rafael Police Department. Do you have a son named Mark O'Hara Chapin?"

"Yes, I do. What's happened?"

"Well, we're holding him here at the police station, Mr. Chapin, and since he's a juvenile we can release him to your custody if you come up here."

"Has he been arrested?"

"Oh yes. We're holding him on a citation."

"What for?" I'd already assumed it was for marijuana.

"Well, your son and two other boys were riding up and down Fourth Street, and they were noisy. Shouting at pedestrians. They were stopped by a traffic officer and he found an open jug of wine in the car."

"OK. I'll be right up."

I made it to San Rafael's police station in twenty minutes. Mark was in a small office, rocking back and forth in a swivel chair. We didn't say hello to each other. He just continued to rock, a silly grin on his face. "He's taking it pretty lightly," I thought.

With Mark was a towheaded boy I had never seen before. On the floor of a hallway leading to a row of jail cells, under the bare, glaring lights, was one of Mark's closest friends. He was a nice, introspective boy with an appalling stutter. Words came from him, after long, painful hesitations, like sudden explosions. He was not stuttering now, however. He was passed out cold. Red wine and vomit covered his clothes.

His mother, having received the same sort of phone call, arrived at the station. She looked at her senseless son on the concrete floor, gathered her well-tailored coat around her, and retreated behind a wall of respectability.

"Why, I had no *idea* he ever drank anything," she said. "Why, he's a *good* boy, he's never been in trouble."

She annoyed me. "Sure he's a good boy," I said to myself. "But that's no guarantee he doesn't drink or that he doesn't smoke pot. It's time you learned of these things." She was trying to preserve the sanctity of her middle-class world; she was trying to absolve herself of blame for what her son was, or wasn't.

Besides, I didn't really believe her.

The mother and I and the newly arrived father of the blond boy, who was named Eric, signed papers and were handed juvenile citations for "Violations of the ABC Act —possession and consumption of alcoholic beverages." We were ordered to bring our errant children to the county probation department for a determination of whether they should appear in Juvenile Court. Mark's friend was revived and cleaned up a bit, and we left the station.

During the ride home I questioned Mark. It was all Eric's fault, he said. If Eric hadn't stuck his damned head out of the car window and yelled at people they wouldn't have been picked up. And it was unfair of the police to arrest him, Mark said; he hadn't done anything bad. Once I caught a minor inconsistency in his story and pointed it out.

"You know I always lie, I lie all the time," he said quietly. It sounded to me like an accusation: he couldn't afford to tell me the truth—the truth in my hands was too dangerous. Or was this just my guilt tuning in?

Mark's arrest, if it had any effect on him, encouraged his belief that one could break the law and get away with it. There was a perfunctory visit to the probation department, where Mark listened to a short lecture from a probation officer who was probably five years older than he was. The charge was dropped, and that was that. I got the impression that Marin County, harassed by the increasing abuse of drugs, was not to be bothered with trivialities like an open jug of wine.

The arrest occurred on March 9, 1965. It was during this month that I started seeing The Owl, and it was during this month that Mark stopped seeing him, "at least for a while." Not that Mark was coping with his problems any better; it was just that we were fed up with missed appointments, with dragging him to the doctor's office, with his repeated claims that the doctor was valueless. I didn't have much confidence in the man either, but, drifting in a storm of my own making and too weak to search for another psychiatrist, I clung to him. I talked, and The Owl remained silent; often I chatted away about things that seemed completely irrelevant, because I didn't like those long, expensive, and unproductive silences.

The Owl would never tell me anything about himself. "Have you ever been divorced?" I asked him once.

"Why do you want to know?"

"Just curiosity, I guess."

But he wouldn't tell me. He sat there and smiled his little smile and kept silent until I stumbled into something else to talk about.

Instead of seeing The Owl, my time might have been better spent trying to find solutions for Mark. He began cutting classes at Tamalpais High, he began going to San Francisco (a noisy, raucous place in North Beach called Mike's Pool Hall was a favorite hangout, and we got several reports that he was seen in the tawdry streets of the Tenderloin), and he began stealing money from us. He was still receiving an allowance of two dollars a week, but obviously it wasn't enough to keep him supplied with marijuana or with acid tabs. He didn't take a lot of money —a quarter here and a dollar there—but his thefts helped to foul the family atmosphere. O'Hara and I took to counting our cash. We hid wallets. We followed him into our bedroom to catch him in a pants pocket or a handbag. It was demeaning.

"What are you doing, Mark?"

"Nothing" (while quickly closing a purse).

"Well, please get out of there. Don't go into our bedroom without permission."

Mark also began to sell his belongings, presumably to pay for drugs. I never saw a transaction, but things disappeared, and once I came across a receipt for an air pistol he had pawned for ten dollars. When we would make such a discovery and ask what had happened, he would reply with his all-purpose sentence, "I don't know."

In the spring of 1965, obeying a sudden impulse, I drove Mark to an expensive store in Mill Valley and let him select an entire wardrobe of his own: mod blue blazer with a scarlet silk lining, flowery shirts, bell-bottom trousers, and black Beatle boots. (Why didn't he like Brooks Brothers clothes, as I did?) The outfit was gone by the end of the year. Not worn out, just gone.

We should have insisted he see another psychiatrist, and we should have found one for him. We didn't. But in

June an event took place that brought him unwillingly
back to The Owl: the Great Marin County Narcotics Raid.

O'Hara and I had been tipped off about the raid by a
Sausalito city official, a friend whose daughter was a frequent companion of Mark's. The raid was to be county-
wide, involving city police departments and state narcotics agents. Undercover men had been making buys for
weeks. Some of the money they used had been supplied by
Sausalito's government, although O'Hara, a member of
the City Council, knew nothing of the plans until we received our tip. The agents were supposed to be aiming at
the biggest dope pushers in the county.

The exact date when the agents were scheduled to
round up suspects was June 5, a Saturday. O'Hara and I
concluded that it would be harmful for Mark to get busted
(we discussed the idea of letting him take his chances),
so right after breakfast on June 5 we got him into the car,
despite his grumpiness and aversion to being waked up,
and drove slowly to Inverness, a town on Tomales Bay,
thirty miles north of Sausalito. Mark was puzzled—why
were we taking him for a ride against his will?—and
kept pleading with us to go home. But we strung out the
day, eating a long lunch at Manka's, an excellent Czech
restaurant. And this must have puzzled Mark even more;
we were getting along with him very badly in those days,
so why the switch, why were we treating him to an elegant meal? We put off his questions, and we didn't get
him back to 16 Cazneau Avenue until five in the afternoon. By then he was more angry than puzzled. He knew
something was up, but what? And there was, admittedly,
an element of fantasy, of weird unreality, to the whole
day. The weather was beautiful, the scene benign, and
here was this nice-looking American family out for a
drive and a pleasant lunch. Togetherness. But this nice-
looking American family was actually hiding a hippie son
from a bunch of narcotics agents. As I drove south into
Sausalito along the waterfront, I looked around for cop

cars, for bearded hippies with their hands held high. There were none.

But the raid had been carried out. The *San Rafael Independent-Journal* was on our doorstep, and the headlines were across the top of Page One. Eighteen persons arrested, some of them teen-agers. Pounds and pounds of marijuana scized. Weapons confiscated. That was a shocker. Was Mark in contact with people who carried guns, for God's sake? Law officers were quoted as saying they had broken up the narcotics trade in Marin, and that any dealers still at large were dumping their stuff in the bay. As I read the story I recognized five or six names— names of Mark's acquaintances—but thankfully none of them, to my knowledge, had been in our house.

Mark read the newspaper report from beginning to end. We told him we had taken him to Inverness to diminish his chances of arrest, and I think we both expected a show of gratitude: "Gee, Dad, it sure was nice of you and Mom to hide me from the narcs." Mark didn't say a word. Instead, he pulled a vacuum cleaner out of a closet, carried it to his room, and vacuumed the floor for twenty minutes. O'Hara and I looked at each other in astonishment. He was removing evidence; he didn't want the police, if they should arrive with a search warrant, to find fragments of marijuana in the cracks of his bedroom floor. He was con-wise.

In the week that followed Mark was more than ordinarily quiet—subdued, morose—and he remained close to home. The raid had scared him badly; he knew too many of the people involved in it, and he put himself into a kind of quarantine.

The quarantine was short-lived. We got a call from Sausalito's chief of police, Kenneth Huck, a man with a crewcut and an air of Germanic efficiency. He assured us Mark was in no trouble, under no suspicion, but that in the interrogation of persons arrested in the narcotics raid, Mark's name had cropped up a number of times. It would be helpful to the police, Huck said, and perhaps helpful to Mark as well, if he were to drop into the police station for a chat. Of course he didn't have to, Huck emphasized, there was no thought of compulsion.

Mark was dead set against it. He felt he was trapped by circumstances and the cops were dangerous, not to be trusted. His instincts cried out to him that he should stay far, far away. But O'Hara and I, talking it over at length, arguing with Mark, arguing with each other, finally decided, hesitantly, that it would be best to cooperate. That's what responsible citizens did: cooperate with authority. So we leaned on him, leaned on him hard, practically ordered him to cooperate; and Mark, too panicky to put up much resistance, went with me the next morning to the police station in downtown Sausalito.

I introduced him to Chief Huck, who sat smiling behind his shiny metal desk. The chief pressed a buzzer and a police sergeant entered the office. Everybody was all smiles—except for Mark, who looked terrified and hateful. With some misgiving I noticed that the sergeant was equipped with yellow ruled paper on a clipboard and a pencil. I thought this was to be a "chat," and I thought that I was to take part in it. I wasn't. I was asked, ever so politely, to wait outside, and the door to Chief Huck's office was closed.

I sat in the chambers of the Sausalito City Council. Morning sunlight filtered through the Venetian blinds, casting shadowy stripes on the floor. Mark's interrogation lasted a half-hour. I could hear nothing. It was very quiet. When the door opened and they emerged, Mark looked thin and defenseless in the company of the two large policemen with their short hair and heavy black boots. Mark was very pale, and he trembled. Chief Huck thanked me: "We sure do appreciate you and Mark coming down here." I glanced at the sergeant's clipboard; he had written a lot of notes.

Going toward the car, Mark walked ahead of me, staring at the street, saying nothing.

"Well, that wasn't too bad, was it now?" I said. It was a stupid remark, made nervously. It was what one says to comfort the patient after a surgical operation. Mark turned on me. He loathed me. He loathed himself.

"It was terrible!" He screamed it out. "They made me tell on my friends. They *tricked* me. It was terrible!"

How do you answer that? How do you tell a boy you've pushed into being a Judas that he shouldn't feel like a Judas? You don't. There is no answer.

When we got home, Mark went to his room and stayed there a long time. He went to his room because he didn't want us to see him cry. But I heard him. He cried for a long time.

O'Hara and I were also upset by Mark's introduction to police methods, and we tried to make amends. One thing we could do was to put Mark in touch with a good lawyer. He could at least be advised of his rights. Mark agreed to this; yes, he would like to see a lawyer. He said that in answering Chief Huck's questions he had revealed the names of several boys and girls unknown to the police, and with every revelation the sergeant scribbled busily on his pad. He was determined that this would never happen again. He was full of self-hate and his anxiety was acute.

We took him to see Frank McTernan, an attorney we knew personally, a member of a San Francisco firm that specialized in civil rights cases. Another member was Charles Garry, who later became famous for his courtroom defenses of the Black Panthers. Both lawyers talked to Mark, and both of them, in reporting back to O'Hara and me, indicated we had agreed much too readily to cooperate with the Sausalito police. Their view was let the cops dig for their dirt, don't hand it to them. But their main emphasis was not on Mark and the law. Mark's legal difficulties were not great; his mental difficulties were. He was a very confused, very sick kid, they said, and he needed intensive psychiatric care, right away.

Mark said all right, yes, he'd go to a psychiatrist

again. His mood, then, was to do anything. And O'Hara and I, choosing the easiest path, hauled him back to The Owl.

We should have made a complete break and started fresh with someone else. Almost anyone else. But we didn't, and in a couple of weeks Mark was behaving exactly as he had before: reluctant to go, skeptical, missing appointments.

Mark's return to psychotherapy was, in our family, the main result of the Great Marin County Narcotics Raid, but there was another, more subtle result: our attitudes toward the police shifted and this added to our family troubles. O'Hara and I moved in different directions. She, more than I, had been a believer in duly constituted authority. She was far from being a fink, but she tended to go to the police, to ask for their assistance, to use them as servants of the citizenry. I had tended to let the police come to me and to be wary of them. Now both of these tendencies were reinforced, and O'Hara and I grew more and more conscious of the difficulties between us as the police became a larger factor in our lives. And Mark was caught in the middle.

As for the Great Raid itself, it didn't do what it set out to do. Pennell told me casually that within a month it was as easy as ever to get drugs in Marin County. It was a cinch to score.

Chapter 9

TAMALPAIS HIGH SCHOOL, according to the gossip, was saturated with drugs: dealers roamed the campus, the only straight students were athletes, everyone else was a head. The fact, then, that Mark himself suggested transfer to another school in the fall of 1965 shows he still had some instincts of self-preservation. He was crazy for drugs —by now a true cultist, he would pop any pill, such as my hypertension pills, into his mouth to see what happened—but he was also afraid of what drugs were doing to him. So he asked for a transfer.

By all means, O'Hara and I said. We'll get you into another school. The idea was not new, but in the past Mark had been stubborn in opposing it.

I wrote to Eastern preparatory schools: Exeter, Andover, St. Paul's, and Loomis. Mark's chances for acceptance were slim (his grades had dropped to C's and D's) but I wrote anyway for catalogues and application forms. In the back of my mind—far, far back, where they would not be exposed to O'Hara—were some negative thoughts about private Eastern schools. Psychiatric bills had put us deeply into debt, and I hadn't the slightest notion where I would raise the $3,500 needed to send Mark, for example, to St. Paul's School. And there was resentment too: I'd gone to a public high school, so why should Mark be treated to a private education just because he used drugs? I looked at the application forms and read the catalogues, but I didn't send in a single application. If I had to, I could always fall back on the excuse, a valid one, that Mark's grades were too low.

I took Mark to Lick-Wilmerding High School in San Francisco for admission testing and he failed. I took him to the Drew School and he passed. Drew's standards were not high and its tuition was nominal—about $500 per semester. Someone said to me, "The trouble with Drew is that it's a place where parents stick their problem children." We stuck Mark in Drew School.

The school building had once been a private mansion. It was on the fringe of San Francisco's ghetto. The rooms were dark, the equipment in poor repair, and the administrators seemed to give off a musty odor—the odor of fatigue and resignation. Mark's dislike of the school was immediate. "But for Christ's *sake,* Mark, we went to all this trouble to get you in there, now *stay* for a while."

He stayed. And for a couple of months he made a real effort to pull himself together. He stopped smoking cigarettes and we praised his resolution. He carried textbooks home and I actually saw him sitting at his desk with the books in front of him. It's true, he spent a lot of time drawing psychedelic pictures in the margins of the pages; but the mere fact that he opened the books was an improvement over his previous semester.

And he even went out for "extracurricular activities." He got a role in the school drama department's production of Edward Albee's *The American Dream.* It was a strange affair. All the actors looked like hippies to me; the teacher-director was (I gathered from Mark) a mystic,

who later flipped out and proclaimed that he was the sun;
and the audience at the play's single performance con-
sisted of hippies and the parents of hippies. Mark was
very nervous on stage, not a born actor, his make-up
crudely done; and I got nervous watching him. His role
as the Father called for him to smoke cigarettes, and that
was the end of his swearing off tobacco. He has smoked
ever since.

A few weeks after Christmas we began receiving
notices that Mark was cutting classes. During the Christmas holidays he said he wished to return to Tamalpais
High. He missed his friends. We said all right, you can
return. Drew School had been a failure, another failure.

One of the things Mark did when he cut classes at
Drew School was to visit a nearby music academy. Soon
after, he asked if he could take drumming lessons. Certainly, I said, I'll be happy to pay for them. But does it
have to be the drums? Guitar, perhaps, or the piano?
A gentler musical instrument? No, it had to be the drums;
and so twice a week he stayed after school and was taught
drumming at the academy. The lessons were inexpensive,
and I was pleased to have Mark show an interest in something, in anything. He practiced every day in his bedroom.
His diligence astonished me. At first he used a drummer's
pad, tapping out sequences from a book of rhythms, de-
veloping his wrists. But the pad was not very satisfying,
and he asked if I would buy him a set of drums.

It was odd that I should skimp in other areas finan-
cially but when it came to drums go to the Acoma Music
Shop in San Francisco, where professionals bought their
instruments, and get the best set available. I was like a
gambler, gambling for Mark's survival and staking all on
those drums. O'Hara expressed her disapproval. Why
couldn't I have bought a "student" set? What if he loses
interest?

Mark and I went to the store together and got the
works: snare, bass, two tom-toms, high-hat, cymbals, a

variety of drumsticks. They were made by Rogers. They gleamed. Miles and miles of chrome and acres of shiny red metal, beautiful German brass in the cymbals. Mark loved them.

I bought them on the installment plan. The purchase price plus interest, insurance fees, and replacement of many lost or stolen parts over the next two years totaled more than $1,200. An investment.

The drums in all their flashy splendor dominated Mark's room. They took on a life of their own; they were like guns—exploding, rattling, thundering guns—making sounds that could wound you. Mark quit his drumming lessons, but he hit the drums every single day. I bought him a large secondhand record player, and his learning method was to play along with rock groups—The Beatles, The Grateful Dead, Jefferson Airplane, and above all The Rolling Stones. He worshiped the Stones, knew every line of every song by heart. In order to hear the records over the roar of the drums, Mark had to turn the record player up to its highest decibel range, which was high indeed. The house throbbed. For at least an hour every day we were battered by sound. Thought was suspended. This usually started in the late afternoon. At six o'clock O'Hara would poke her head out of the kitchen and scream, "*Supper's ready!*" I would climb the stairs and, bracing myself, open Mark's door.

I can see him now: pure concentration, his taut thin body curved over the drums, the sticks held lightly in his long fingers, his hands darting here, there, his foot pumping the bass pedal, his lips moving with the lyrics, his face flushed. He was in another world, he was in London, he was a Rolling Stone, on his way to fame and wealth.

I would move in front of him, catch his attention, and signal. He would put down the drumsticks, turn off the record player, and come to supper. I was amazed and delighted at his progress, and told him so. I never complained about the noise. I hoped, half-hoped, that the

drums and Mark's commitment to them, the firmest commitment he ever made, would lead him away from drugs.
But then at the *Chronicle* one day I met Marty Balin, top
guitarist and singer with Jefferson Airplane. You had to
be very careful in the rock scene, Marty said; drugs were
part of it. If you were serious about your music, if you
wanted to make it, you had to be very careful. Marty said
he knew lots of young rock musicians who were "wasted"
already on drugs. I wondered about my son.

Through the spring and summer of 1966 Mark continued to improve on the drums; and he was soon involved
in proposals for the formation of a new rock group. The
organizer was a guitarist with cocker-spaniel eyes and
long, stringy, unwashed hair. His mother was a believer
in health foods and his father was seldom home. He was
shy and gentle, not the sort of kid you'd think capable of
organizing anything, but he was dedicated and he worked
at it. I liked him. The other musicians were Mark on
drums; on bass guitar, a smart-aleck, blustery talker
whom I neither liked nor trusted; the son of a prominent
and liberal Mill Valley family on electric organ; and a
pudgy little girl singer. Or rather, they were the charter
members of the group; its personnel tended to change,
depending on who was available.

I was completely in favor of this enterprise and said
I would help them whenever I could. In helping them I
discovered that fledgling rock groups exist by weathering
a series of linked crises. Theirs is not an easy existence.

The first crisis for the group was what to name it.
The name had to be selected with the utmost care. It had
to be attractive, to have drawing power; it had to "sound
like the name of a rock group" (a nebulous requirement);
it had to be acceptable to all the musicians. Scores of
names were suggested and then dropped. Arguments
were unending. The original name—at least the one they
first settled on—was The Third Rail, which to me sounded
nice, neat, and catchy. I endorsed The Third Rail, which

was thereupon replaced by Purple Haze. I said that was
OK too. Then one day Mark said that finally they had
agreed on the absolutely perfect name.

It was "Rebirth Spreading Forth."

Mark explained to O'Hara and me at the supper table
that "Rebirth Spreading Forth" was a quotation from The
Tibetan Book of the Dead, or an allusion to it, or something like that. The Book of the Dead was currently very
big with hippies; Mark frequently referred to it. The name
was guaranteed to make their rock group known the world
over.

I should have said it was a marvelous choice, and
Mark, not one to respect my aesthetic tastes, would have
perversely gone back to the group to argue for still another change. Instead, I said it was terrible, it reminded
me of a placenta, it was too abstract, too hard to remember, and too long to fit into a rock-dance poster. A short,
snappy name was what they needed. Mark pointed out
that it was his rock group, not mine, and retreated into an
injured silence. But I had wrecked his enthusiasm for
the name, and this was needless. What difference did it
make really? Why couldn't I just shut up?

"Rebirth Spreading Forth" lasted quite a while, but it
never freed itself from argument, and eventually it was
abandoned. The final name, under which the group got a
few rock-dance engagements, was The Magenta Raindrop.
Not bad, at that—and I had had nothing to do with its
choice.

Finding a place to rehearse was even more troublesome than finding a name. If one drummer can make a
big noise, one drummer and one amplified organist and
two amplified guitarists can make an intolerable noise.
All the homes of all the musicians in The Magenta Raindrop were tried out for rehearsals, and the results were
discouragingly the same. Neighbors phoned the police;
the policemen arrived at the door and said they were sorry
but to knock it off, no more electronic rock.

I was afraid that if it didn't have a place where it

could rehearse undisturbed, the group would fall apart.
At best, it would be held together by loose strings, and I
very much wanted it to stay together. I wanted Mark to
keep busy. I tried to rent a shack in the country. I talked
to men who owned warehouses or lofts at Gate 5 and
Gate 6, the ramshackle industrial areas north of Sausalito.
Without exception, my appeals ("Maybe they can use your
place at night when nobody else is using it") were denied
on the grounds that this was a bad risk. Rock musicians
are hippies, these men said, and hippies are careless, and
careless hippies mean fires from cigarettes.

The Magenta Raindrop, with me as their guide and
sponsor, became nomads traveling the length of Marin
County's bay shoreline in search of a haven. I shall never
forget one of the havens we found—a house surrounded
by tall fir trees in a deep ravine. A pimply youth named
Claude was our host, by virtue of his parents' absence.
We carried the musical instruments down forty rotting
wooden steps to the house. When we opened the door,
the stench was appalling. The house was overrun with
cats—they crouched under chairs and stared at us—and
the floor was littered with shit and half-empty cans of
cat food. It made a grotesque studio. But The Magenta
Raindrop practiced there for two weeks, until Claude's
mother showed up. Mark said you kind of got used to
the smell.

The more I acted as chauffeur for The Magenta Raindrop, the more they took me for granted. Especially Mark.
It was hard labor to pile those musical instruments into
the trunk and back seat of my car, and often they would
expect me to pick them up at a moment's notice. I began
to resent them, to begrudge their requests. But I hated to
give it all up. This was my project, my scheme for
"getting Mark involved"; and to scrap it now would be to
admit defeat, and also to admit that O'Hara's skepticism
was well founded. The atmosphere got tenser and tenser.
One muggy summer day, I hurriedly gathered up the
drums and, with Mark riding silently beside me, drove to

Brown's Hall in Mill Valley. The Magenta Raindrop had a dance engagement that night, and they had suddenly decided to rehearse beforehand. Mark and I unloaded the drums in front of the hall. Sweating, feeling martyred, I stood on the sidewalk while Mark, without a word, turned to join his friends inside.

"Hey, aren't you even going to say thanks?"

"Thanks," he said, with his back to me.

"You sonofabitch," I yelled after him, and he vanished.

On the same night I watched him play—the only time I saw him as a "professional." Mark had indicated fairly strongly that he didn't want me around when he was playing a gig. He said it would inhibit him, and I suppose he got thoroughly stoned before he picked up the drumsticks. But O'Hara and I had been asked to chaperone this dance, and we accepted. The lights in the hall were low, and Mark, on stage, was barely visible. I could just see his hair, flopping up and down as he drummed, and occasionally I could hear his voice raised in a hoarse, Mick-Jaggerish shout. The music was ragged, I thought, but the kids on the dance floor seemed to be with it, their faces set and solemn as they danced. The amplifiers were at full volume. O'Hara wore cotton plugs in her ears and winced in time to the music.

The next day I praised Mark's performance. He said he and the others were paid five dollars each, but that was only the beginning. His expectations were boundless. He talked about how they were going to rent a bus and tour the country. They were going to cut a record. He asked me to approach Bill Graham, the rock impresario, to see if there was any chance of an engagement at Fillmore West. Bill Graham sighed, in a resigned way, and said he could have his pick of a million rock groups like The Magenta Raindrop.

In the end, all it amounted to was disappointment and bitterness between O'Hara and Mark and me, and more drugs. I am reasonably certain that Mark, after some of the dances, got paid off in drugs rather than in money. What did it matter to him? One was as good as the other.

He began missing rehearsals. The leader would phone the house. "I'm sorry, I don't know where he is." And he began lending his drums to other boys. He called it lending, but I suspect he was compensated—with a few joints, or perhaps some Methedrine. Because he was now into Methedrine, into speed. In a small way, at first, but into it. Pennell, among others, told me he was fooling around with it. When I questioned Mark he said yes, he had taken it once, in a cup of coffee.

He stopped playing the drums in his own room. He was hardly ever *in* his own room, or in the house with us at all. The drums, when they were not on loan, stood silent, a monument to his failure. And to mine. They kindled my resentment. I would go to the head of the stairs, look at those drums, and wonder where Mark was.

One evening, when he had been gone for days, O'Hara and I arrived home about nine o'clock after a movie and a stop at the No Name Bar downtown, and my resentment exploded. I put the car in the garage and, going inside, heard O'Hara call to me. She was in Mark's room, and so was Pennell.

"There's a boy here who says he's going to borrow Mark's drums," O'Hara said.

"The hell he is." Anger rising, I took the stairs two at a time. The "boy" was tall, shaggy-bearded, roughly clothed, and a stranger to me. He looked a lot older than a boy. He was standing beside the drums.

"Now wait a minute. Who said you could take the drums?"

"I said he could," Pennell answered. "He said he'd talked to Mark about it."

"Well, I don't want him to. I don't know him and I have no way of keeping track of the drums."

"They belong to Mark, don't they?" the youth said.

"That's right, they belong to Mark. But I paid for them."

"Now, calm down, Bill," O'Hara said. I could feel the drinks.

"What's your name?" I said.

"What difference does it make?"

"OK, that does it"—my voice getting higher and higher—"you fucking well know my name and I don't know yours. You can get the fuck out of this house and don't you ever come back."

The four of us clattered down the stairs, and I pursued the youth into our driveway.

"You're the one ought to be in the loony bin," he shouted.

"I'm not scared of you, you sonofabitch. Come back and say that."

He jerked off his sweater and came back. He hit me once with his open hand on the side of the face, and it felt wonderful. Exactly what I wanted, a good stiff jolt. For a few moments it changed all my bitterness and anger into action. But I kept my hands at my sides (instinct warned that he could clobber me in a real fight) and this disarmed him. He couldn't swing at someone who refused to swing back. "Aaaagh, you're crazy," he said in disgust, and got into his panel truck and drove off.

After that, it was too painful to look at those shiny red drums, which were once full of promise. They were a visible reminder that my son and I were so far apart that it was like a disease. I had bought the drums hoping they would bring us together; now they just stood there, silent and impotent.

I took the drums to the Acoma Music Shop. The proprietor asked no questions. He gave me a hundred dollars and apologized. Used drums, he said, were a dime a dozen.

I got rid of Mark's big old record player too. I gave it away.

Chapter 10

THE REPORT CARDS at Tamalpais High School provided spaces for teachers' comments—spaces that customarily are ignored. On Mark's June, 1966, report card, adjacent to a column of pathetic grades, D's and F's, was a comment. "It has been very sad," wrote his history teacher, "to watch this boy go down the drain."

Yes, but the history teacher did not realize that Mark still had a long distance to go before he would reach the bottom. And neither did I.

By now, I suspect, he was using LSD regularly, not just experimenting with it. One day he told his psychiatrist, who relayed the information to me, that he'd taken thirty trips, another day he said more than a hundred. I doubt if Mark himself knew. To us he was saying no trips at all. Oh no, he never used acid. Not any more.

But the first signs of the kind of mental disorientation that often goes with LSD were evident. His memory suffered lapses. His handwriting became crabbed and shaky. He would laugh when there was nothing to laugh at. He would turn on the gas stove to heat water for tea; ten seconds later he would leave the house. He began to leave cigarettes burning on the edges of tables and bookcases, and O'Hara and I developed a chronic fear of fire.

He was more listless, more withdrawn from the immediate sights and sounds around him. He would sit in the living room staring at the wall, smoking, not even listening to a record.

"Hey, Mark. Wake up. Why don't you go for a walk, or do *something*?"

"I dunno."

We had never given Mark many chores to perform. He had few duties during childhood. Now, whenever we asked him to mow the lawn or to pick up his room, he did it so badly that it had to be done over again. He didn't care. People who drop acid are said to lose their egos. (And Dr. Timothy Leary, in my view an irresponsible and destructive man, a reckless Pied Piper, maintains that this is a good thing.) Acid heads lose more than their ego. They lose their self-esteem. They lose their "being."

So it was with Mark. He was also losing what little identification he had with O'Hara and me. He was attached to us for food, shelter, and clothing. That was all.

We knew that LSD was taking him away from us. Yet we had never actually seen him in the full throes of an LSD trip. He was still careful about that; he went on his trips in the homes of friends or on the beach. What we got was the aftermath—the confusion and the fatigue.

That's where we were when the school year ended in 1966, and O'Hara and I, unhappy, tense, and tired— tired of the messiness of our life, tired of trying to care for Mark—decided that a vacation was essential. We had to get away. I had skipped my *Chronicle* vacation in 1965 out of deference to the sports column, so I had six weeks coming to me. We decided on Mexico. And Mark would go with us. There was a slim chance that it might help him; moreover, we had little choice. We shrank from leaving him with relatives (we were, in truth, ashamed of him), and to leave him behind, alone in the house, was out of the question. He could never care for himself. Pennell, by this time, was living with friends. She was now an independent young woman, secure in the knowledge that she did not need to lean on her parents for emotional or financial support. The turning point had been a six-month trip to London, where she got a job in a boutique on Carnaby Street. As a child Pennell had been shy. That shyness gradually faded, and when she returned from England it was completely gone. She had grown up; but in growing up she became closer to O'Hara and me, because now we were equals.

O'Hara and I planned to drive to Mexico City, with three- or four-day stops along the route. It would, we hoped, be a cheap vacation—we were dead broke. We told Mark of our plans and he was surprisingly agreeable. I'm not sure why. He couldn't have looked forward to being cooped up in an automobile with his parents for six weeks. But a lot of his hippie companions had traveled in Mexico. They grooved with its earthy, peasant virtues, I guess; it was real, it wasn't plastic like the United States. And there was plenty of pot there.

At any rate, Mark said all right, a trip to Mexico would be cool, and we arranged to leave on a Saturday in July. On the previous Thursday I wrote a sports column and thought, "Well, I won't have to worry about *that* for six weeks, what a relief." Friday evening Mark said he was going to the Fillmore to hear Jefferson Airplane. If we had ordered him to stay in he would have sneaked out of his bedroom window, as he had before; so we said yes, go to the Fillmore, but please be home early, tomorrow's going to be a busy day. At eleven o'clock we went to bed. At midnight Sergeant Tom Zink of the Sausalito police

phoned to say that Mark and three other boys had been
arrested in Mill Valley on narcotics charges. The other
boys, he said, were being taken to Juvenile Hall. But he
would be willing to pick up Mark in Mill Valley and bring
him home. (Mark, after all, was the son of a Sausalito
city councilwoman.)

As I got out of bed and dressed, grumbling and swearing, I thought, "Mark may be in poor shape, but he retains
an astounding ability to fuck things up." What I should
have thought was, "It proves how sick he is."

We waited in the living room, outraged and silent.
Mark and the sergeant came in the door, and the ser-
geant, seemingly embarrassed, muttered briefly and left.
Mark headed for his room.

"Wait a minute."

"I'm sleepy."

"Bullshit! You're sleepy! The least you can do is tell
us what happened."

"What good will that do?"

"Now just sit down." Both of us were raving at him.
"What in hell are we going to do about our vacation?
You'll have to appear in court, and God knows when
that'll be."

"It wasn't my fault. I wasn't doing anything."

"I don't care *whose* fault it was, goddammit! I can't
change all the plans now. I can't change my vacation at
the *Chronicle*."

Mark shrugged and looked at the floor, as if to say,
what's the point of arguing with a maniac?

We dragged the story out of him. One of their tail-
lights was out, that's how it all started. This nosy Mill
Valley cop stopped them at a street corner, while they
were driving back from the Fillmore concert, to tell them
a taillight was out; and he smelled the pot, and he
searched the car, and he found some joints, and he busted
them.

"It wasn't my fault they had joints in the car."

"Were you smoking marijuana?"

"Yeah, but I didn't have any *on* me."

"Did you tell the cop you were smoking?"

"Yeah, I did. I told them at the police station."

Mark said they had handcuffed him, hands behind his back. Angry as I was, I couldn't see why cops should put handcuffs on my sixteen-year-old son.

It was two o'clock in the morning and we all went to bed. I felt trapped. Mark's court procedures might take weeks. The courts were jammed. How could we possibly go to Mexico? Fucked again. He must have done it on purpose, spitefully.

The next day I phoned Mark's psychiatrist. He said it might have been better, psychologically speaking, if Mark had been shipped off to Juvenile Hall with his fellow culprits. He was a bit doubtful when it came to this preferential treatment.

Mark himself seemed wholly indifferent. He was guiltless. He moped around the house while I got more and more angry. Then he asked if he could go downtown. I said, "No, goddammit, you stay here, you've caused enough trouble."

"How're you going to stop me?"

"I'll show you how," I said, and phoned Juvenile Hall.

"My son's been arrested on a marijuana charge," I said to the man who answered my call. "I'm bringing him up. I want you to take him into custody."

There was a rather long silence, while the man tried to figure out what was going on. Here it was late Saturday afternoon and some idiot was playing cop with his own kid.

"Well, I don't think we can take him. Not just like that. Not unless he's out of parental contol or a danger to himself or others."

"He's out of parental control," I said. He wasn't, in fact. He was standing in front of the fireplace, staring at me, too dumbfounded to move.

"Well, if you insist. Bring him up here, then, and we'll see what we can do."

It occurred to me that if Juvenile Hall refused to accept Mark I would look awfully foolish. But there was no turning back now. We drove to "the Hall," a collection of low buildings, most of them in the Spanish style, surrounded by a high fence. It appeared to be pleasant enough, not at all menacing. Then, when he climbed from the car, Mark put on a quick little fit, flailing about with his arms, kicking the air, and rolling his eyes. It was his way of saying, I felt, that his father was plainly crazy. And his mother too, because she was with us. There's no explaining why he got into the car in the first place.

We waited in an office. Mark made no attempt to escape. In a half-hour we were joined by a young probation officer who did not hide his displeasure at being saddled with an awkward chore at the end of the week. He didn't waste much time.

"You know, you could be in a lot of trouble," he said to Mark. "This is your second arrest—that's right, I looked it up—and if the judge wanted to he could put you in here for quite a while.

"But I'll tell you what. We'll keep you here over the weekend. If you shape up, if you show a real change in your attitude towards your Mom and Dad, if you cooperate with us, then you can go to Mexico with them. If you *don't* shape up, we'll keep you here longer."

An excellent solution, I thought—of dubious legality.

We left him there and returned Monday morning. When a matron brought Mark to the office I felt a sharp twinge of pain and sorrow. He was wearing faded dungarees and a coarse gray shirt. He was in prison garb.

He glared at us when we said hello. He could not believe, could not *believe* what we had done to him.

The probation officer said Mark's behavior had been fine over the weekend, he had worked hard and was free to go. I think the probation officer wanted to be quit of the whole situation. Somehow it was peculiar, twisted.

We drove silently out the gate and headed for Sausalito. I decided to make a friendly overture.

GARDNER WEBB COLLEGE LIBRARY

"What was it like, Mark? How'd you make out?"

"It was shitty," he said. I decided that now was not the time for a friendly overture.

Tuesday morning we piled into the car and departed for Mexico, and a jolly vacation party we were, too.

The trip was a failure, and the roots of its failure lay in the fact that Mark was not part of us. He was merely carried along, another piece of the luggage.

While we were on the road, Mark showed scant interest in the countryside, except to say repeatedly that he hated the buzzards hovering high in the Mexican sky. They made him think of death, he said. He amused himself with the car radio. The most popular song of the month was "Little Red Ridinghood," one line of which is climaxed by an orgiastic scream. Mark invariably screamed along with the singer. We got sick of that.

O'Hara suffered terribly from the heat. I hadn't bothered to buy an air conditioner for the car—they cost about $350—and the dry Mexican desert air, like the breath of a furnace, knocked her down. Mile after mile she rode with a moistened washrag on her face.

In Mazatlán, O'Hara and I had a nasty fight over Mark. Drinking cocktails in the Hotel del Playa, she accused me of being needlessly cruel, of baiting him.

"Aw, fuck it, let's call the whole thing off. Let's go home."

"Bill, don't say that. Why not give it a try? Why not *try* to make it work?"

"Fuck it. Let's go home."

"Bill, you're a hard man to live with."

"I am? OK, I am. You want to try living alone?"

Cocktails finished, we ate a glum and silent dinner.

In Tepic, Mark took a walk by himself on the main street and returned to our hotel room frightened, his face pale, his chest heaving. He refused to say what had happened. Maybe he tried to buy marijuana and the transaction got rough. But I'm only guessing.

In Guadalajara, we all caught the tourista and retained it for the rest of the trip, more or less.

In Mexico City, the Hotel Polanco's boiler blew up and we had no more hot water. The toilet leaked on the floor.

Those were the highlights of our trip.

Unaccountably, Mark and I shared one pleasant evening together in Mexico City. O'Hara, down with the tourista, was in bed early. I took Mark to see a James Coburn movie, *Our Man Flint*. It was full of psychedelic gimmickry and bright colors. Mark enjoyed it; he laughed when there was something to laugh at, for a change. Afterward we went to a bar and drank Tom Collinses. The idea of being able to drink legally excited him, and we chatted about all sorts of things. Mark promised to get back to his drums, to start going to his rock group's rehearsals. We discussed his future in music. I said he had a lot of talent, and believed it. I felt close to him—a rare feeling those days—and I think he felt close to me. But it was brief, a flicker of warmth in a crowded bar in a foreign city. Our love had no staying power.

And yet shortly after the trip he made another gesture toward me.

On the drive back to Sausalito, we stopped overnight in Reno, Nevada. We were within the circulation area of the *Chronicle*, and my first act after checking into the motel was to buy a paper and turn to the sports pages. When we had left Sausalito, the space where my sports column ordinarily appeared contained the sentence, "William Chapin is on vacation—his column will resume on his return." The sentence had been dropped. I had been canned. Thumbs down on the column. I was sure of it. I had seen it happen to other columnists.

When I finally showed up in the *Chronicle* office, it took me five days to confirm that my column no longer existed. The column didn't run in the paper, but no one wished to administer the *coup de grâce*.

"That was a shitty way for them to do it," Mark said to me. He meant it too, and I was glad to have his sympathy.

A couple of weeks later Mark's marijuana case was dismissed. Insufficient evidence.

Chapter 11

*I*T WAS A STRUGGLE to keep Mark in Tamalpais High during his senior year, and we lost. We had long since surrendered any hope that he would go to college, but we still believed that a high school diploma could be valuable to him. Some day it might help him get a job, if he were willing and able to work.

Frequently, of course, he was not at home, which meant that he was not in school either. When he *was* home, we flung the covers back, boosted him out of bed, fed him, bossed him and jawed him and yelled at him. Fought with him. It was like fighting a shadow.

"Hurry up, Mark, you're going to miss your bus. For Christ's sake, get moving, I don't want to have to drive you up there again today."

"Mmm. OK. Can I play a record before I go?"

He sat in his classes, on occasion, and his teachers complained. They said he was disruptive. He bothered his classmates. He fell asleep. He stared at the ceiling.

100

He mumbled to himself. He was, in the unanimous view of his teachers, his counselor, and the Tamalpais dean of boys, a weak student.

And he continued to take dope. His closest friend, now that he had drifted away from The Magenta Raindrop, was the very black, sensitive, and hyperintellectual son of a middle-class Michigan family. He was "interested in film." He wanted to make an avant-garde movie, and he migrated west to Sausalito because of the town's free and untrammeled spirit. Everyone hung loose in Sausalito. This young man and Mark were often together, in the Tides Bookstore, in the little downtown park where the bongo drummers drummed. After a while he, like Mark, wasn't much interested in anything at all. Except dope.

In March, 1967, the dean of boys called to say that Mark had been suspended for two weeks. He regretted the necessity, and so on and so on, but Mark was cutting too many classes. In a subsequent conference with the dean, O'Hara and I reached a decision to remove Mark from school completely. Indefinite suspension, said the dean of boys, might shock our son into a realization of what he was doing to himself.

It didn't shock Mark, but it embittered him. He blamed us. He hadn't *left* school, his parents had pulled him out of school. "You guys," he liked to say, goading us, "have turned me into a dropout. I'm a high school dropout." It was a convenient excuse. It took him off the hook.

When Mark was suspended, he was still seeing The Owl, and the doctor's reaction to the event was revealing. Recently—perhaps three weeks before the suspension— he had spoken in glowing terms of Mark's progress— progress that was best illustrated, he said, by Mark's new attitude toward school. He had really resolved to apply himself, to stop goofing off.

Maybe so, said O'Hara as she sat in the doctor's office, filling in for one of Mark's missed appointments,

Maybe so, but Mark just got suspended. Indefinitely.

The Owl smoothly executed a sharp U-turn, without ever raising his voice. Somehow, Mark had refused to play fair, had conned him, betrayed him, and it was time to end the relationship. (I had already stopped seeing him.) He said he could no longer help Mark and, further, that we ought to consider putting him in a hospital. The boy was seriously disturbed.

That was the last we saw of The Owl, and there was no follow-up from him, no serious inquiries about Mark's mental health, or mine. Once, at the bottom of a bill (I still owed him hundreds of dollars and was paying off the debt by the month), he scrawled three words: "How is Mark?" I think that's what he wrote. The handwriting was so small I could hardly read it.

My feelings about The Owl are mixed, and obviously not objective. I don't think he improved my mental health, and perhaps no one could have improved Mark's; but his presence, if nothing else, was a calming influence. He helped me weather a storm. And it was not altogether his fault that I did not seek out a psychiatrist who would be more compatible.

Where did we go now? No school, no psychiatrist, and a recommendation that Mark enter a hospital.

The dean of boys suggested Continuation School. Courses designed for students who were short on credits were held at night. Continuation School had a low status in the community; it was for second-raters, for losers. The idea of sending Mark there was repugnant (it challenged my snobbery), but we could not bring ourselves to the belief that he was at last at the end of the educational road. We persuaded him to try it. He was too depressed to resist; the full impact of his failure was beginning to hit him.

Twice a week, at 7 P.M., we drove Mark to Tamalpais High and waited in the car to retrieve him after his hour of instruction. There was no conversation during these trips. It was as though we were carrying a bale of straw to the school and dumping it in the doorstep. Then one evening he didn't return to the car when the hour was up. I searched for him, walking through the corridors, poking my head into classrooms. No Mark. I left the school and saw him running toward the car. He had tricked us. Night after night he had ducked out a back door of the school, gone to a friend's house, presumably to blow pot, and then returned. When he confessed to this, sullen, miserable, yet still defiant, I screamed at him so loudly he jumped in fright.

"What do you think I am, driving you up here? I'm not your fucking slave!"

That was his final day in Continuation School.

Meanwhile, O'Hara and I sought medical advice. Despite our lack of confidence in The Owl, despite our disillusionment, perhaps he was right, perhaps Mark did need to go to a hospital. Though how were we going to pay for it?

We were still members of the Kaiser Health Plan, in the *Chronicle* group. I got an appointment with Kaiser's Dr. Solomon Cohen, a physician who specialized in adolescent problems. I described, at length and as accurately as I could, Mark's accelerating use of drugs and his present condition. I said he was strongly opposed to hospital care but maybe, if we could get him admitted, he would change his mind.

Dr. Cohen heard me out. His answer can be summed up this way: "I understand and deeply sympathize with you, Mr. Chapin. But unfortunately it's been our experience that these youngsters reject treatment. In particular this applies to the ones who have been using amphetamines. They don't think they are sick. And from what you say, this would include your son. I'm afraid it wouldn't work. We could admit him but he wouldn't stay. I'm sorry."

I thanked Dr. Cohen and got up to leave. He patted me on the back.

I got an appointment with Dr. Robert Wallerstein of Mount Zion Hospital, also a psychiatrist. He was smooth and urbane, and his sympathy was the equal of Dr. Cohen's. So was his answer: "We can't take Mark because he wouldn't stay here."

O'Hara got an appointment with Dr. Leon Epstein of the University of California's Langley Porter Neuropsychiatric Institute: "I'm sorry, Mrs. Chapin, treatment is voluntary here. We don't have any locked doors and your son wouldn't stay. He'd run off in a week. That's what happens with most of these drugs kids."

We checked with Marin General Hospital, which said it had no in-patient facilities for drug addicts. We checked with Ross General Hospital, which said the same thing.

I visited Synanon House in northern Marin County. I was impressed by the humanness and dedication of the former junkies who ran the house. Obviously they felt that Synanon had saved their lives and could save other lives. But they were skeptical of Mark. You've got to be practically crawling on your hands and knees when you get here, they said; you've got to have an awful desire to kick it, if Synanon's going to work for you, and that doesn't sound like your boy, does it?

No, it didn't sound like my boy.

The walls seemed impregnable. I wrote in desperation to Dr. Norman Garmezy, psychology professor at the University of Minnesota and a friend from our Worcester days. "Please, Norman, what the hell are we going to do? I mean *what the hell are we going to do?*"

Norman Garmezy put us in touch with Dr. Sheldon Korchin, a clinical psychologist at the University of California in Berkeley. Again I made my presentation. "Not exactly my field," said Dr. Korchin, "but I do know a man here, a psychologist and therapist, who is working with a number of kids like your son. He seems to have a special empathy for—well, for the disenchanted young, for the hippies. He might be just your man. His name's Bill Soskin."

We arranged to meet Dr. William Soskin in his office on the Berkeley campus. It was easy to see why he had "a special empathy," because he looked like a flower child himself, slightly gone to seed. We gave him the full story, and he nodded and nodded and nodded. He was quite familiar with the story; only the name was different.

Dr. Soskin said that in his opinion the span of adolescence for Mark's generation was much longer than it had been in the past—kids didn't grow up until their mid-twenties. In our affluent society they didn't have to; they were much more sheltered. I said I agreed with him. He said this extended period of incubation was probably a good thing; it led to greater security. Thinking of Mark and how often I had wanted to be rid of his problems, I said I wasn't sure I could agree with him on *that* one.

Dr. Soskin said he was engaged in a study project on teen-agers' neuroses. In connection with this, he was seeing boys and girls therapeutically in his Berkeley home, and Mark might be fitted into the schedule. I said that would be fine. Dr. Soskin did not mention a professional fee, and I failed to ask him what he charged. Money was crass. Besides, this was a research project; perhaps it was free.

He inquired if I had ever taken LSD, since LSD had figured largely in our discussion. I said no, never, nor did I intend to take it. I said I thought it was dynamite. "Have *you* ever taken it, Dr. Soskin?"

"Oh, yes. I took it once. Under controlled conditions. I felt I needed to know what it was like. You know, to understand it."

He inquired if I had a sense of failure as a parent.

"I sure do. A great sense of failure."

"Well, I think that is too bad. Really. From your description, you have instilled in Mark some very decent values. It's not your fault those values don't equip him to live in American society. He's against war, isn't he? Against Vietnam? You wouldn't want him to be a hawk, would you?"

I didn't answer. I thought the point was far removed from Mark's profound, drug-induced illness, and I wasn't too certain I liked Dr. Soskin. But where could we go? Perhaps Mark would respond to him.

As O'Hara and I were leaving, Dr. Soskin said he was gratified to find that I was not the person he had visualized when I phoned from the *Chronicle* office for an appointment.

"Oh? How come?"

"Boy, you sounded like a Four-Star Final reporter on the phone. You know: Bang! Bang! Crack! Crack! All business."

I said I was surprised; most people complained that I mumbled when I talked. I decided that Dr. Soskin hadn't met very many Four-Star Final reporters.

On several successive Saturday mornings, I drove Mark across the Bay Bridge to Dr. Soskin's lovely home high in the Berkeley hills. The doctor talked privately with Mark and then invited me to join in at the end of each session. Our conversations were tentative, soft, deliberately non-medical. Dr. Soskin used no psychiatric jargon, and I approved of that. But his therapeutic approach was to identify as closely as possible with his teen-age patient, and there my doubts grew. It was all very well to be anti-Establishment (I was anti-Establishment too, and had been for years), but did the therapist have to become a hippie himself to save someone from them?

I have forgotten almost all of Dr. Soskin's remarks during therapy; they were too vague, too elusive. I remember this statement: "You ought to really *listen* to the lyrics of Jefferson Airplane. Have you ever really *listened* to 'White Rabbit'? It's enough to make you cry."

My car radio had frequently provided me with the lyrics of "White Rabbit," a song about mind-bending drugs, and they hadn't made me cry.

And I remember this exchange, when Mark and I were both in his living room:

"You've mentioned your drinking, Mr. Chapin. That must have had some effect on Mark."

"Well, I'm not sure how much he's been aware of it, how much he's seen me drunk."

"What about it, Mark?" Dr. Soskin asked, turning toward my son. "Does your father's drinking frighten you?"

"Sometimes I'm afraid he might hurt himself," Mark said.

His comment jolted me, because I wrongly believed he had never seen me when I couldn't walk properly.

Dr. Soskin announced one day that he had to go to Washington on a special assignment and would be gone a month. I think Mark was more relieved than distressed by this news. When the three of us were together, I got the impression that he answered most questions as if he were being imposed on. Above all, he seemed remote. And I felt, in truth, that Dr. Soskin was applying sweet gentle therapy to a grave disease. "You don't," I said to myself, "paste a band-aid on a severed jugular vein."

Before he left for Washington, Dr. Soskin sent us a bill. Because it was partially unexpected, it seemed staggeringly large (actually his rates were no higher than The Owl's), and there was no listing of dates, of appointments. I felt I was being charged by a man I was not completely comfortable with for a series of Saturday morning chats. I asked for and eventually got an itemized bill, which I paid, and we did not see Dr. William Soskin again.

Now what? Same old dilemma, same old dead end.

My *Chronicle* vacation was near (I was now a general-assignment reporter). Would we risk another of those exhausting adventures like the Mexico trip? Would we try again to solve the problem of what to do with Mark Chapin, if only for a few weeks? Yes, we would.

A year ago we had been too ashamed to try relatives, but not now. I wrote to my father, who lived by himself in Noank, Connecticut. My mother had died in 1965. My father was eighty-two years old, a New England eccentric, a warm and loving person. He had not seen Mark in six years. Would he, I asked, take Mark into his house for a month while O'Hara and I visited friends on the East Coast and went to Expo '67 in Montreal? I didn't level with my father. I didn't tell him that Mark used drugs. I was scared to. I merely said he had the usual quota of adolescent problems.

My father said yes, of course, he would be delighted to see his grandson.

We plunged ahead, thrusting aside what we knew, deep down, was the case: that Mark was much too sick, much too unmanageable, to be foisted off on my father. I got the plane tickets. I arranged for Gerri Lange, a *Chronicle* colleague, to move into the house with her three sons while we were gone. Gerri is black, and fairly militant about being black. She said she'd love to have a vacation in Sausalito, away from the city. I felt smug in giving her the opportunity to do so.

Flight day was Monday. Saturday morning Mark declared that he was not going and there was no way we could make him go. He was old enough to take care of himself. What right did we have to drag him against his will to the East Coast? He was afraid to fly.

It was the Mexican ploy all over again, complicated this time by our promise to Gerri Lange. For two days we argued, ranted, reasoned, pleaded, threatened, denounced, and bribed. It was on again, off again, on again. Gerri said don't worry, she understood. By Sunday evening we seemed to have it settled—Mark said he would go—but the atmosphere in the house was very tense and shaky.

After supper O'Hara began to pack our suitcases. Mark asked if he could go to the Tides Bookstore in downtown Sausalito and I, like a fool, said, "Yes, but be back in an hour." He left. I looked in on O'Hara. She was sitting on the edge of the bed, and trembling.

"Jesus," she said. "Oh Jesus, I'll bet he's taken off."

"He'll be back," I said.

O'Hara rocked her body to and fro. "Oh please, Bill. *Please* go see if you can find him."

I found him in five minutes. He was walking toward home, with a friend at his side. They were both laughing; not a care in the world. I beckoned him, and he got into the car. I told his friend it wasn't a good time to visit our house.

When I walked into our bedroom, O'Hara hadn't moved. "He's here," I said. She started to scream and strike her thighs with her fists. I tried to put an arm around her and she jumped up and pounded the wall. And she kept screaming "All I want is peace—peace —peeeace—*a little peeeace!*"

It was the first time I had ever seen O'Hara, in twenty-six years of marriage, give way to full, unbridled hysterics, and I was more embarrassed than sympathetic. It was awkward. What would the neighbors think with all this screaming going on? Should I slap her face, as they did in the movies? I did nothing but sit on the bed and wait.

Tired out, spent, she was finally quiet, and we went to bed. I was relieved to find Mark still in the house when we woke the next morning.

During the taxi ride to the airport and at the airport I watched Mark as if he were a Federal prisoner. Minutes before they announced our flight, Mark said he had to go to the men's room.

"I'll go with you. I need to go too."

"No, you wait outside."

He disappeared and I posted myself, like a U.S. marshal, at the men's room door. He was gone for what seemed like a century. Reflecting on it now, I'm certain that he went in there to swallow Methedrine, and that he had gone downtown the night before to get Methedrine. He needed his fix; he was afraid of flying.

He sat in a window seat of the Boeing 707. He asked a stewardess for a Seven-Up and spilled most of it on his trousers. He stared into the sun and the clouds. He kept moving his right hand in front of his face, brushing away cobwebs that perhaps he could see but I couldn't. We landed in Boston, on a sweltering day.

"Well, how was it?" I asked my son.

"It was interesting," he said.

Chapter 12

Our decision to fly to the East Coast with Mark proves in itself that O'Hara and I were afflicted with a kind of blindness, for only a blind person would have stumbled into such an incredible labyrinth.

From the Boston airport we took a bus to the beautiful old home of my brother and sister-in-law, John and Lois, in Fayville, which is not far from Worcester. The plan was to have a family reunion there for a couple of days; then Mark would accompany his grandfather to Noank while O'Hara and I went to Montreal, where we would stay with O'Hara's mother. Already it was too complicated.

Everyone greeted Mark warmly and tried to put him at ease.

He smoked incessantly and was silent, withdrawn into himself. My father (I was shocked to see how much he had aged) was also silent. Here was his grandson with long, unkempt hair and messy clothes and a pained, faraway vision in his eyes. Could they ever know each other? My father had surely read about hippies and the California scene, but had he ever been exposed to them?

After supper there were drinks on the back porch as it grew dark, and Mark, who was barefoot, said he was going for a short walk. It was a long walk, and he returned to the house in the rear seat of a police car. Nothing wrong, the officer said, but he spotted this shaggy, barefoot kid on the highway and thought he might be lost. Fayville is a small, well-to-do, conventional community, and the policeman reacted to Mark in a small, well-to-do, conventional way. But to Mark it was harassment.

The next morning my father was gone, without Mark. He left a note to my brother John; it said he felt awful, but it wouldn't work, he was too old to "adjust" to living with a boy who "looked so bizarre." Later I phoned him to say it was all right, don't worry, and he sounded close to tears. What a selfish thing to do, to put an old man, my own good father, into a position that would make him cry!

Mark was outwardly impassive when I told him my father had left, but he was nevertheless wounded, and in the months to come he often mentioned it. "That was weird, the way he took off like that. I guess he didn't like me."

It was time to change direction. If we were lucky, if we hit upon the correct path, we might emerge at the far side of the labyrinth. A family conference, centering on Mark but without his participation, went on into the night. A bottle of Scotch was drunk.

We rejected the notion of taking Mark with us to Montreal. O'Hara's mother, Clare, was a sweet old lady who lived in an expensive Montreal apartment building and put a great stock in appearances. Everything had to be "nice." If my father, with all his eccentricities, could not accept Mark, then dumping him on Clare Fontaine was beyond the pale.

O'Hara and I desperately needed to be quit of him for

a while. We needed to be by ourselves. Yet we couldn't
leave him with John and Lois—they both worked.

John and Lois had a summer place, a small farmhouse in backwoods Vermont, and that, finally, was our
solution. On the weekend we would drive up there;
O'Hara would continue to Montreal while Mark and I
stayed at "Joe Hill," as it was called. We would rough it.
If I couldn't stand it or if Mark couldn't, we would fly back
to Sausalito.

Mark must have felt like a pariah, unwanted and
alone. We made a few flimsy efforts to cheer him up.
Lois joked and joshed him, but he refused to laugh.
John gave him rudimentary guitar lessons. O'Hara and I
visited the Harvard campus with him and worried that he
might somehow score.

He had another unpleasant encounter with the Fayville police. He said he was picked up and 'questioned at
the police station, then released.

"What do you think of the people around here,
Mark?" asked Lois, by way of starting a conversation.

"They're fucked," he said.

A few hours before we were due to leave for Vermont,
newcomers arrived. Bruce and Tanya Mackay drove up in
a battered and smoking Mercedes-Benz. Tanya, a tall lovely
girl with a Modigliani face, was distantly related to the
Chapins by marriage; and Bruce, a folk singer and composer, was her new husband. They were young, bright,
hip, and easygoing; they led a gypsy life in New York
City, and to Mark they were friends come to the rescue.
At last, someone he could talk to.

The Mackays were headed for Montreal, where' Bruce
and his folk-music group were to appear at Expo '67. They
agreed to stay overnight with us at Joe Hill, and Mark
rode to Vermont in their car.

His spirits rose a degree or two, though he was careful
to put on a doleful face when we were around. He walked
in the woods, played with the Mackays' big white Sam-
oyed, and talked for hours on end with Tanya, who liked

to indulge him. Sunday evening he appeared at the door of the room where O'Hara and I had slept. We were re-packing suitcases.

"Can I go to Montreal with Bruce and Tanya? They said I could stay with them. Can I?"

"Oh, Lord. Mark, we can't switch plans again. It's just too complicated. I thought it was all set for you to stay here with me for a week or so."

"Please. Bruce and Tanya said I could. They said I wouldn't be any trouble."

He sounded like an eight-year-old pleading for a piece of candy. I said to myself, "He's spoiled; we dance to his every tune."

We gave in, naturally. I handed a fifty-dollar check to Bruce, as expense money. Mark squeezed into the rear seat of the Mercedes with the dog and the musical in-struments, and they were on their way to Montreal and Expo.

There was no longer any point to my staying at Joe Hill, and that night in Montreal we tried to explain the whole tangled mess to O'Hara's mother—why her grand-son was in the city in which she lived but couldn't meet her. It wasn't easy. She had no inkling that Mark was on drugs. From O'Hara's letter she knew he was a hippie, one of scores of hippies in Sausalito. And she had con-cluded, out of her boundless store of unworldly in-nocence, that a hippie was a homosexual. Because, in her words, he "swung his hips." She listened now, with a kind of marvelous come-what-may acceptance, and that night she "included Mark in her prayers." She has been praying for him ever since. It seems to work as well as anything else.

Bruce, Tanya, Mark, and the musicians in Bruce's group were strewn about Montreal in hippie crash pads. After the Expo performance, the Mackays were to return to New York, and that would leave Mark homeless again. We were still determined to keep him away from O'Hara's mother. I bought plane tickets to Sausalito for Mark and me, and phoned Gerri Lange to advise her, again, of an early eviction. O'Hara would stay on in Montreal.

We saw the Expo gig. Mark set up the instruments and the microphones. They played in an outdoor theater to a skimpy audience of French Canadians, tourists, and nuns. Even Mark played, or at least he banged a tambourine in listless fashion. The sound equipment was terrible, and the applause that followed their three numbers was weak.

O'Hara and I went backstage to offer our dutiful congratulations. We approached Mark, who was standing alone, smoking a cigarette.

"Bruce and Tanya said I could go to New York with them and stay in their apartment if you'll help out with some money for food."

Well, why not? All the resistance was knocked out of me. Why the hell not?

We got Mark identification papers through a notary public; I canceled the plane tickets and gave the Mackays a hundred dollars, with a promise of more when it was needed. On the eve of their departure for New York, I talked by phone to Tanya.

"Is Mark using any drugs, that you know of?"

"Well, a couple of times he's said, 'I sure wish I had some speed,' but he hasn't done anything about it. And *we* certainly haven't given him any. He'll be all right. He's really a very nice kid."

They left, and O'Hara and I spent two quiet, restful weeks in Montreal and in the country at Clare's summer cottage. We returned to Sausalito via Vancouver. Gerri Lange said she'd had a wonderful time, and moved out of the house.

Mark was 3,000 miles away. O'Hara and I felt as though a huge weight had been lifted from our shoulders. We hoped he would remain 3,000 miles away for months and months. We didn't write to the Mackays—why stir things up? If the visit were going badly, we would hear about it soon enough.

Two weeks passed, two weeks of freedom. Then we got a telegram from Bruce Mackay: MARK TAKING PLANE HOME. PLEASE SEND $187 FARE IMMEDIATELY. I wired the money to New York.

The next day we picked up Mark at the San Francisco airport bus terminal. He was near the curb, a guitar at his feet, and he was wearing a ragged jacket I had never seen before. He got into the car.

"Hello, Mark. How are you?"

"I don't want to talk."

"Did Bruce and Tanya kick you out?"

"No."

"How come you took a plane instead of a bus?"

"I don't want to talk about it."

Five days later we got a long letter from Bruce. It described what it was like to live with Mark in a New York City flat. And it offered some advice. Here is the letter:

Dear Bill and O'Hara:

First of all, and it's really last of all, our apologies for the switch in transportation plans, but once Mark had decided to go (it was his decision, not ours) it seemed the best thing that he leave as soon as possible, and his need to get to California (his inner sanctum utopia) we thought we should try to satisfy as soon as possible. The increase in transporting costs was about $40 and we thought that (a) you could afford it and (b) originally he was going to fly back with you anyway.

Mark's visit with us to a large extent was an exercise in frustration which sometimes threatened to get the better of us but I don't think it ever did. His exposure to my particular musical situation appealed to him but also put him uptight, due to his insecurities concerning his own talents as a drummer, due to his insecurities concerning his own talents as an individual.

When we arrived in New York Mark lay on the couch a good deal. On the second day he went out with Jasmine [their dog] to go to the store. He disappeared, and after a lot of worry on our part, we finally found him five hours later in the park. He had got lost, and had walked around a good deal of New York in a kind of paralyzed panic. Before he left the house he was given specific directions and a map, and a small amount of money. When he discovered he was lost, he neither thought to phone us or to take a taxi home, and the people from whom he asked directions consistently misdirected him, which I feel is slightly more Kafka-esque than real.

Now we tried to dictate some terms of our living arrangement, terms which most people don't need to be told. Things like: When you live with people you must take some responsibility for making the unit function. You must be aware of the fact that people are interested in your presence as long as you are interested in them. And that there is also some work which always must be done by someone, and it's easier for everyone if everyone does a little of it.

Mark consistently agreed with the above and consistently avoided doing anything about it, which was a drag, because what happened was that Tanya or I would say "do this" or "do that" and he would usually perform badly the function. Now whether he performed badly or not is not really important. What seems to be important is in what spirit did he perform. But he never seemed to care.

Example: He badly wanted a guitar. So I said OK. You want a guitar. We don't have any money. Look up the used instruments in the yellow pages. Find one and price one. You want a guitar. You get it. Make sure it stays under $20. What happened was that we all went for a walk and found one in a pawn shop for $13. It was a good guitar with a broken neck and was a good buy. But the guitar had to be fixed. Mark, who wanted to play the guitar but didn't want to fix it, worked on me to fix it. Our rationale in a situation like that was: If he *could* fix it, he *would*. Something keeps him from functioning which he can't control. So Bob Sanersen took Mark to a repair shop where he bought the materials to repair the guitar and Bob and I worked on the guitar, and often Mark didn't even watch. Now repairing that guitar was time-consuming but not difficult, and I started my relationship with guitars four years ago by fixing one.

At any rate, the guitar was fixed, and all it needed was good strings. Mark made no effort to go out and buy them although he asked me to. Finally I gave him the money and he went out with Tanya and by coincidence they met Cyril who actually bought the right type of strings. Mark asked me to put them on, and I refused. I ended up putting on three strings and making him put on the rest. From which point he was with the guitar a great deal and seemed to enjoy it.

At which point we moved to a basement apartment which was much bigger and decidedly a much better place for three people to live. But it was in a dreadful state of disrepair and there was more cleaning up to do than you can imagine. We worked very hard and Mark was a problem because if I asked him to do something it generally meant more work for me than if I had just done it myself, but we both felt it was the best thing for Mark to be made to work, and occasionally it seemed that we were right. Sometimes, he would go to bed tired after a day's work, rather than tired of the world, if you know what I mean. During this time we tried very hard to get into his head and discover what he really thought of anything. And often we thought we did. Which made for some gratifying moments. But let me say that Mark generally distrusts his own vision to such an extent that he believes he will either be laughed at or just not believed; and of course there is something else, which could be perhaps explained by saying that the world in Mark's head is very exclusive and other people are not really included in it.

The following points for your consideration:

1. We have friends some of whom have gone through what Mark has gone through (and everybody does, to a greater or lesser extent). And some of the people Mark met here have gone through a great deal, and have important things to say. But Mark was unable, or did not wish to relate to them, which was definitely to his loss, which brings up the question of death wish and that sort of thing, which also everyone has, to a greater or lesser extent.

2. His interest in music is very restricted. It can be summed up by saying that he is only interested in his own head in a very limited sense. e.g. "I refuse to accept the fact that anything that anybody says is of value and of interest to me, other than those things I can *directly* relate to —like The Grateful Dead or The Rolling Stones." Which is not a state of enlightenment.

It is obvious that Mark goes through a lot of pain and is usually more uncomfortable than comfortable. The question is: if he can't put a stop to that, who can? The answer does not exist, but I feel that everybody, in some way or another contributes. I do not consider his stay here a failure in any way. Sooner or later he will discover that when you hit the same stone wall with your head again and again, that perhaps some of the fault is in yourself. Mark is the hero in his own saga as we all are to ourselves, but the real hero is someone who can discover that there are more truths than one's own, and that in some sense, that is where it's at, so to speak.

When Mark couldn't take the moving scene any longer he developed a fever and went to bed very unhappy, and a change of scene was called for, so he went to the country for a few days with some of our friends, and stayed with a group of people who are dedicated to building a community in the country and making it self-sustaining. Mark was there for four days and waited for food to be brought to him, and contributed nothing. The people there are quite tolerant but he would have been kicked out very shortly, because, to revert to Gilbert and Sullivan, he was not pulling his own weight.

3. Mark has a habit of coming over and reaching into your pocket for a cigarette, again and again. If you give him a package of his own, it is gone in no time and the hand starts reaching into the pocket again. The same principle holds for the refrigerator. If something special and expensive is waiting to be shared perhaps at the dinner table, Mark will have disposed of it before that time. When made aware of this, Mark seems to think somewhat like Jasmine. e.g., "I have been told not to eat all the yogurt or drink all the beer today. This does not apply to anything else, or to the beer and yogurt tomorrow." He seems to have to relearn for each case.

My feelings about Mark, and they are Tanya's too, are difficult and easy to describe. He is two people and probably many more. What I consider a "together" person is someone who can take all of his "selves" and make them all act for his benefit, understand them all and groove with them. Sometimes Mark is a kind, warm and very endearing person. It is those qualities which make it possible to live with him at all, because sometimes he definitely has a sense of humor about himself and makes you know it. Qualities like Laziness, Selfishness, Pigheadedness, and other Victorian adjectives are not really qualities which I can attribute to people with any clear conscience at all, knowing to some extent that when I am those things it is not because I really *want* to be them at all, but somehow or other, I can't help it.

But it is a tough world. And in order to cope with it, it has to be grappled with and not totally avoided, I think.

I think Mark has been spoiled. Things seem to have been too easy (or have they really been too difficult?). If I were asked to actually presume to give advice, I would say, kick him out. Give him no financial help. You should only help in areas where he seems to want to achieve something, like go to school or take lessons or something. I don't value school systems very highly or the values which most people seem to think important. But if Mark is thrown into a situation where he is forced to come through on someone else's terms, I think it would be the best thing for him.

Another thing. Mark would not dare to talk to me the way he sometimes talks to you. He wouldn't because he realizes that I have an objective power which you as a father do not have. From my own experience, my father does not relate to me well at all, as you probably know. I consider you and O'Hara to be in somewhat better shape than my parents, but as you know about yourself and I know about myself, we are not perfect. I think that you must come to terms with the past you and O'Hara and Mark have had and realize that blame is a bad word and right *now* is the most important thing.

Mark is very advanced in some ways and is not a child in those ways. Patronizing him is lethal. Perhaps forcing him to be an adult in every way is the best and most painful thing to do.

Mark left New York because he found it too tough, and we were not in a position to force him to do anything. When he broached the matter of returning to California, he said he would like to go back to school or try to get into a university. We said instantly, "Then go." And that rather frightened him. But I think he wanted to go back because it would be easier and I think you should not contribute to make it so. Mark is in love with himself in the most indulgent of ways —perhaps because he thinks no one else is. A good kick in the ass would make him hate the kicker on a short-term basis, but on a long-term basis should be appreciated. To what extent do you think you have let him get away with murder?

You would probably find it difficult and painful to let Mark out on his own to become a zombie hippie flower child of San Francisco, but I don't believe anything could be worse than his present situation, and that conceivably he could be forced to come to terms with himself. Right now he dislikes you because he needs you so much; he needs you to fill his pockets, iron his shirts, tell him he's a good boy by your acceptance of the situation in any way, and I believe to a certain extent he has you over a barrel, a barrel of half-love and half-chickenshit. It is true to say, "But he is our son." But it is also true to say, "He is a person separate from ourselves. How does he shape up with the rest of the world as a non-son person?"

Tanya and I are well and going to Montreal in a week. Please feel free to let Mark read this if you feel it necessary and accept our best wishes in this matter and our love.
                                    Bruce and Tanya

Mark read the letter. He made an odd little gesture of dismissal with his hand and said, "Well, you know, Bruce and Tanya—they don't know where it's at."

Chapter 13

I KICKED HIM out of the house. With no money, with a pasteboard box containing his messy clothes, or what remained of them. Sink or swim, Mark. Go stay with your drug friends and see how *they* treat you.

This was in September, 1967, when most children are returning to school. In August he had had his eighteenth birthday. The eighteenth is supposed to be significant, another step toward manhood. It made me ache to see him go, and it made me lie awake at night.

Nevertheless Mark, through steady deterioration of his personal habits and his hygiene, had managed to make his banishment slightly easier than it could have been. He was on a lot of speed now (despite his denials) and his deterioration was typical of the speed freak. Speed freaks simply don't care any more. It takes a long time to become addicted to the amphetamines, in contrast to the opiates, but when a person is finally trapped, he tends to forget about his "wasted" body. He is superior to the flesh, he has risen above it. But he made O'Hara and me acutely aware of his body:

"Mark, don't eat your boogers like that." He would explore his nostrils with an index finger, stare at the slimy little nugget as if hypnotized by it, and then eat it. He especially liked doing this at the dining table.

"Mark, go back upstairs and put on some *clothes*, god-dammit." He would emerge from his room without a stitch on, or we would find him standing naked in the living room looking out at the street, or he would leave the house with his trousers clinging to his hips. "Mark, goddammit, you'll be arrested for indecent exposure. Nobody's that much interested in seeing your balls—what's the matter with you?"

"Mark, don't leave the kettle boiling." Again and again and again he would heat water for tea or milk for cocoa and forget it ten seconds later. Again and again and again O'Hara cleaned the stove or disposed of a blackened kettle.

"Mark, don't piss on the toilet seat." He would walk into the bathroom unzipping his trousers and let fly, spattering urine all over the toilet and the floor.

"Mark, butt your cigarettes. For Christ's *sake*, you'll burn the house down one of these days." Every piece of furniture in his room was scarred with burns. Often when he finished a cigarette he balanced it upright on its filter tip. These untidy little pillars dotted the entire house; O'Hara kept removing them.

"Mark, *please* chew with your mouth shut." It was disgusting to watch him eat. He stuffed great gobs of food into his mouth, using his fingers as fork and knife, and chomped noisily. Semi-liquids like mayonnaise dribbled down his chin. He used his sleeves as napkins.

"Mark, go to bed, please go back to bed, it's three o'clock in the morning. And stay out of the icebox." Coming down from speed, he was terribly restless, pacing, pacing, pacing, unable to sleep, opening the refrigerator door to see if there was anything he could grab. He drank from the juice pitcher and gnawed at the leftover steak.

My conversations with Mark were by now limited to ill-mannered injunctions and oaths. And what did he have to say to me? Things like, "My sexual relation is in a state of fifteen—Hell's Angels Graduate Club."

"Now what does that mean, Mark?"

"It means I came out of a mother."

Or, "Last night when I got into bed I pretended I was under water—like those Inca—mmm—Inca Inca Inca things."

"I don't understand you, Mark."

Or, "George Harrison got into my head last night and pretended I was Judy Witherspoon."

"Who's Judy Witherspoon?"

"I don't know."

So I kicked him out of the house, as Bruce Mackay, only a few years older than Mark, had suggested. I had support from the younger generation. It gave me the strength to do this thing I found very hard to do.

He was back in a week. In mid-afternoon he knocked on the locked front door. I wasn't home, and O'Hara answered the knock. He was filthy, he smelled, his trousers and legs were smeared with shit. He was in fact physically ill; he had become ill apparently from eating rotten food, and lost control of his bowels and come home for some motherly care. He could not have been too far away, actually. What was O'Hara to do, shut the door in his face and hope he would go? She couldn't. She took him in and cleaned him up. He was put to bed, and he said he was going to stay off dope because dope had fucked his head. He wouldn't or couldn't say where he had lived, or with whom. "You know. Around."

He was fed wholesome food, and he got well—that is, physically well—and in no time we were right back where we had been before I kicked him out. *Mark, put on some goddam clothes!*

Often, when he was coming down from speed and not sleeping, he was as irritable as we were, and he had some screaming fits of rage. We locked our bedroom door at night. We were scared of him. We locked the windows so he couldn't climb into the house if we both were away for a few minutes. We never left him in the house alone for any length of time.

I tried to get him to register for the draft. I said he could be a conscientious objector—I would provide the legal assistance—or he could get a physical rejection or whatever, but at least he ought to register. I pointed out that unregistered he was subject to arrest. But he couldn't face it. Once he let me drive him to Selective Service headquarters in San Rafael. As we approached the building he began to tremble. "Stop the car," he said, shaking all over. I stopped and he tried to get out. "OK, Mark, it's OK. We won't do it if you're that frightened."

Once he said he didn't have to worry about the draft because he was "a little bit gay."

"You are? Have you had any homosexual experiences?"

"I don't know."

"Well, have you or haven't you? You sure as hell ought to know."

"I don't know."

"Well, it's not the end of the world if you have. Lots of people have had homosexual contacts without being real queers."

Once, when I was reading in the living room and he was sitting there doing nothing, living in his interior world, he suddenly said, "You know what people say to you in this town?"

"What do they say, Mark?"

"They come up to you on the street and they say, 'That's what you get for suckin' a nigger.'"

"What do they mean when they say that?"

"I don't know."

In the tone of his voice and in his face there was a loathing that was total. Was he making this up, I wondered, or had it happened? His expression told me that it had. But Mark would never call anyone "nigger," and his bitter use of the word now was directed at those who did.

One evening he asked me to take him to Bob Dylan's movie, *Don't Look Back*. I said sure, I would. Before we had reached the outskirts of Sausalito, he said, "What theater is it at?"

"The Presidio."

Immediately he started to tremble and to brace himself against the car seat as if warding off an attack. He thought I meant the movie was at the military Presidio in San Francisco, which meant soldiers—and death—and the war in Vietnam.

"Let's go back," he said, and I turned the car around. I started to cry softly.

"What's the matter?" he asked.

"Oh Mark, Mark. You're so sick. You're so goddamn *sick*. What's going to become of you?"

He was embarrassed by my crying and couldn't wait to get out of the car.

Our search continued even though we had no precise definition of what we were searching for—a medical solution? a miracle? *any* termination?—and all the while Mark got rapidly worse. When he wasn't out somewhere on a speed trip, he retreated into his bed. It required an ugly, name-calling battle to get him up.

I took him to see Robert Mogar, a psychologist at San Francisco State College. Mogar, according to a *Chronicle* colleague, had established an unusually close rapport with young people. He had made himself an expert on the draft and served as informal counselor to students. We went to the old Victorian house he lived in, in the Mission District of San Francisco. There were Tibetan

God's Eyes in the windows, an elaborate hi-fi with piles
of records, and a tall brass candlestick on the coffee table.
To Mark these were sympathetic signs, and he and Bob
Mogar talked easily and at length.

"Why do you take speed, Mark?"

"Well, I don't know. It's the flash, I guess. It feels
good."

"Is it like sex?"

"I guess so. I don't know."

"Have you ever shot it, or just taken it orally?"

"Just orally."

Mogar said that shooting speed was far more dangerous than swallowing it. Later I looked for needle tracks
on Mark's arms (he rolled up his sleeves quite willingly)
and found none.

Mogar said he was working with a self-disciplined
drug program called The Family at Mendocino State
Hospital and that he would be glad to take Mark there
for a visit, or he would rap with Mark again in his own
home. But I didn't push hard to continue the relationship,
neither did Mark, and nothing came of it. Mogar never
sent me a bill, which made him unique among the psychiatrists and psychologists we had seen.

One day Mark, so taut and jittery he couldn't stop
moving, agreed to visit a Synanon House with me. He was
ready to try *anything* that would help bring him down
from speed. So we drove to Marshall, in northern Marin
County, to look at Synanon.

The director was a swarthy, 270-pound ex-junkie from
New York City. "Jeeze, the kid's fulla all kinds I don't
know *what* kinda stuff," he said to me after holding a
long conference with Mark. "And he's scrawny, he ain't
eatin' enough. He don't know where his head is, at all,
but he says he'll stay here. We'll give him a try. But he
don't *hafta* stay. It's strickly up to the kid."

I said my wife and I would be extremely pleased if
Mark stayed in Synanon.

"We'll clean him up, first. We're givin' him a haircut right now. The boys are workin' on him."

The director said that Synanon was now forced to charge rates, based on ability to pay, and we settled amicably on $200 a month. It was all very casual. I wrote out a check for one month and left without saying goodby to Mark.

Two miles down the highway from Synanon I noticed a roadside pay phone and called O'Hara. "He's going to stay," I said. "He's really going to stay, this time."

"Thank God," said O'Hara. "I'm so thankful." I could hear her voice break. We were both ready to drop.

That night we had a quiet dinner, with a fine red wine, and talked of new hopes. I told her how impressed I was by the atmosphere at Synanon. We went to bed early, and slept.

At 11 P.M. there was a knock on the door and we got up. It was Mark and a young man who introduced himself as Juan. They had arrived from Synanon in a pickup truck. The first thing Juan did when he came in the house was to give me the $200 check.

"He wouldn't stay," Juan said. "I talked to him all the way driving down here; I really *leaned* on him. I told him he didn't know what it was like to be a junkie like I was. I told him he was throwing away his life."

Mark looked very different. His hair was shorter than it had been in years, almost a crewcut.

"Why wouldn't you stay, Mark?"

"I didn't like the way they treated me, the way they cut my hair."

"But why, *why*? Christ, Mark, you had a chance there, a real chance to get well."

"I didn't want to be all that square."

"All right, goddammit, you don't want to be that square. Then you can take care of yourself. If you can't stay in Synanon, you can't stay here either. Where do you want to go? Got any ideas?"

"How about Morningstar Ranch?"

"All right, I'll take you to Morningstar. *Right now!* Go upstairs and get a sleeping bag from the attic. You're not going to sleep here tonight."

He was startled, and so was I. He had expected to spend the rest of the night in his own comfortable bed. Morningstar Ranch was a hippie commune in the woods, seventy miles north of Sausalito. It was created by a musicologist as a haven from and answer to the materialistic society. The musicologist, Lou Gottlieb, claimed that no one was turned away from Morningstar. It had received some bad publicity; it was reported to be loaded with hepatitis and dysentery.

Mark got a sleeping bag and we left, only a few minutes after Juan left for Synanon. I kept checking the map but I couldn't find Morningstar. Finally I stopped on a dirt road where, I estimated, Mark would be within easy walking distance of the commune. It was about four o'clock in the morning. Not a word had been uttered during the entire trip. I was afraid that any attempt at conversation would have ended with my hitting him.

"OK, you can get out here," I said. "My advice is to bed down in your sleeping bag beside the road, and when it gets light find a farmhouse and ask where Morningstar is. They ought to be able to help you find it."

He got out of the car. It was chilly, with a thin ground fog.

"Goodby, Mark," I said. I wasn't tough enough to let him go without saying goodby. He didn't answer, and I drove away.

He showed up at the house three days later, minus his sleeping bag, and of course we let him in. He was very hungry, and O'Hara fed him. He filled the house with the odor of rancid sweat.

I shall never be certain whether he actually reached Morningstar. I doubt that he knows himself. His stories varied. He was, I believe, beginning to hallucinate without the use of drugs, and being abandoned on a country road at four in the morning could have been enough to send him into orbit.

He said he would like to try Jap Flats, a hippie campground in Big Sur that was regarded by permanent residents of the area as a fire and health hazard. I fitted him up with another sleeping bag (secondhand) and put him on the Greyhound bus from San Francisco to Big Sur. This time he lasted a week. When I retrieved him, late at night in the bus station, he looked truly crazy. His eyes were wild and haunted. He refused to talk about Jap Flats.

He said he would like to try living with Pennell, who was renting a house in Fairfax, a bucolic Marin community, with two other girls. Pennell and her friends hesitated, then gave their assent, and he moved in. He slept on the living room floor, like an ailing pet.

Pennell brought him back on the bus. There was a pathetic stand-up conference in the kitchen during which Pennell tried to explain to Mark as gently as possible that it hadn't worked and wouldn't ever work; and Mark, within his terror and confusion, came to realize that he had lost still another option. Even his sister, his dear, compassionate sister who loved him, could not accept him. "Can't you help me?" he said, leaning against the kitchen sink. "Won't you please help me?" His appeal was not to Pennell alone. It was to me, to O'Hara, to Pennell, to anyone who would listen, to the world.

I drove Pennell back to Fairfax. Mark asked if he could accompany us, just for the ride, and I said no, he couldn't.

"There's absolutely nothing going on in his head right now," Pennell said. "Nothing at all." And in defeat she too wept.

Not long after that Mark clumped downstairs one morning with his right hand pressed against the left side of his chest. "Something's wrong with my heart," he said.

"I doubt it," I said, "but let's find out anyway."

I was able to get an appointment that afternoon with Dr. William Haynes, our current family physician. Haynes called me into his office after he had examined Mark. "His heart's all right," he said. "But how long has he been like this? I haven't seen him in quite a few months, you know."

"He's been getting steadily worse."

"Bill, he's going to hurt himself. You've got to get him into a hospital. Right away. I think the best thing is for me to recommend commitment and then you can get a judge to sign him into Napa."

Mark and I went home. O'Hara and I hardly discussed it. I had already sensed—though I kept it way in the back of my mind—that it would come to this, and she must have too.

It took a couple of days for Dr. Haynes to arrange for papers that would authorize the Sausalito Police Department to escort Mark to the Marin County Courthouse for a commitment hearing. Then, on the morning of December 5, 1967, a sunny warm morning, Captain James Wright and Sergeant Tom Zink arrived in a patrol car. I looked at the heavy wire screen that made the car's rear compartment a small prison, and I thought, "Mark is going to be behind that screen in a few minutes."

The two officers sat down, awkward in their heavy boots, clearly feeling intrusive and anxious to get it done with. Mark was still asleep. I woke him and got him dressed and downstairs. Dazed, smoking the first cigarette of the day, he sat on the couch and peered into the fireplace. He had no idea what was happening. The policemen's uniforms didn't seem to faze him. Captain Wright read the authorization paper, handed Mark a copy, and tried to explain. Mark paid no attention. Once he walked into the kitchen for no apparent reason, and Sergeant Zink quietly followed him to prevent an escape via the back door. "Already Mark, poor old Mark," I sadly thought, "is, for the police, a potential fugitive."

He got into the rear compartment of the car without resisting. "Where we going?" he asked absently. O'Hara and I trailed the patrol car to San Rafael.

Much of the day was spent waiting in a corridor outside the chambers of Superior Judge Joseph Wilson, who had a crowded schedule. The waiting was interminable. Mark smoked, ate candy bars, and talked to himself. He was upset, a little petulant, but he didn't know why. Two court-appointed psychiatrists arrived, one of them young, the other a fragile old man. They interviewed Mark in the corridor. They concluded—what else?—that our son was a danger to himself and therefore was a proper subject for commitment to a state mental hospital for treatment of drug addiction.

The hearing before Judge Wilson was mercifully short. He listened to the psychiatrists' opinions, signed the commitment papers, and spoke to Mark. "You're too valuable a person to destroy yourself this way," he said. "I'm sorry, but I've got to put you in a hospital where you can get well."

A sheriff's deputy, a big beefy man who behaved as if he did this sort of thing every day (and I suppose he did), took Mark by the arm and led him to a holding cell. He told O'Hara and me we might as well go home. He said Mark would be driven to Napa State Hospital in an ambulance, and that it would be sensible for us to wait a a week or so before we visited him, so he could become "acclimated."

O'Hara and I drove home. I wanted, oh I wanted very badly, to get home before I started to cry. I didn't make it. It's lousy to cry while you're driving sixty-five miles an hour on Highway 101.

Chapter 14

O N THE AFTERNOON of December 24 O'Hara and I drove to Napa to join Mark in the celebration of his first Christmas in a mental hospital. We carried inexpensive gifts: clothes and fruit, a carton of cigarettes, candy bars, paperback books of poetry. The gifts had been gaily wrapped by O'Hara.

It was a nice day. The air was crisp and clean after a recent rainstorm, and the dairy cows, grazing slowly in the green Napa hills, seemed part of a peaceful world. But I dreaded the visit, as I had dreaded my only previous visit to see Mark in Napa State Hospital. I was still ashamed of his presence there. My own son in the nut-house, how could that be? And now, on Christmas Eve, our delivery of a few little gifts in a locked ward would be a cruel mockery of life and of the very idea of happiness. But O'Hara thought that not to at least go through the motions would be a surrender to total despair.

We arrived at three o'clock and hurried past the old

men and women, the geriatric cases, who sat in the reception room talking to themselves and waiting to die. We rang the buzzer outside the door to Mark's ward, Q-7, and a fat, matronly attendant with a ring of keys dangling from her waist let us in.

"Hi," said O'Hara to the attendant. "How's Mark?"

"Oh, you're Mark's mother and father, are you?" she said. "I'm sorry to have to tell you this, but Mark's not here. He's escaped."

"Oh, *no*," said O'Hara. "No, no, no."

We stood against the wall of the long dark hall that led to the patients' dormitories. O'Hara looked very small. She held the packages tightly to her breast. Sick people shuffled past us in the hall.

"When did it happen?" I asked.

"Just a few hours ago." She looked at her watch. "It was during the lunch hour. But you know, we were kinda worried Mark might try something like this. Couple of times he tried to go over the wall, so we wouldn't let him out of the exercise yard. This time he got out through the kitchen."

"But why didn't you *phone* us?" O'Hara said, the pain and fear spreading in her face.

"Well, we hoped they might get picked up and brought back, or maybe even come back on their own. They do, sometimes."

"They?"

"Yeah, there was two of them. Mark and a Negro boy, Steve."

"What's Steve like?" I asked.

"Oh, he's a real schizophrenic," the attendant said. "I'm afraid he's not very stable."

I knew what she meant; I remembered him because he seemed sicker than the rest, an incredibly skinny kid, always silent, with lifeless eyes.

"Any idea what direction they went?"

"Most likely San Francisco. The Haight-Ashbury. Steve's from somewhere around Los Angeles but he doesn't really have a home. It's easy enough for them to hitchhike. You'd think folks would know this was a mental hospital and when they pick up kids like that they'd bring 'em back. It don't usually work that way."

"Come on," I said to O'Hara. "Let's go. There's not much chance of it but if we leave now we might see them on the road."

We drove south on the highway that goes past the entrance of Napa State Hospital. It was not our usual route, but it was the one that Mark and Steve would probably have chosen. I drove as fast as I dared to, thinking, "He's an escaped mental patient—but you only read about escaped mental patients in newspapers, you don't *know* them, they're not *related* to you." We didn't see them. They were long gone. But who had given them a ride, and would he treat them gently? They were weak, timorous human beings, not fiends.

Back home again, I phoned the hospital and appealed to the ward attendant to give us any glimmer of news, whatever time of the night. And then we let our imaginations take over. We didn't talk much, we just imagined: he had got to a source of Methedrine, he was hurt, abused, arrested, or dead. There was a wide choice.

O'Hara had invited Frank Chesley, a bachelor friend, and his girl Kathy to share Christmas Eve dinner with us, and she declined to cancel the invitation. I went into the kitchen once when she was preparing the meal. She was almost doubled up, as though someone had struck her in the stomach, leaning against the kitchen sink, and her eyes were wet with tears. "I am having a very bad time," is all she said, and she resumed her work. I knew she was afraid that she would fall apart if she stopped.

The dinner was superb, as were all of O'Hara's festive dinners. Frank Chesley suggested that we all go to the No Name Bar for a nightcap. O'Hara, in an astonishingly calm voice, said no, Mark had escaped from Napa State Hospital and we ought to stay home in the event of a telephone call. It was unreal and horrible to hear my wife give this excuse for not going to the bar for a drink.

We did not sleep that night. In the morning I went to work, and from the *Chronicle* office I phoned one of Napa Hospital's top administrators, a man whose chief mission in life seemed to be the spreading of good cheer whatever the circumstances. I had talked to him before; he was incessantly ready to agree with anything I said.

"Oh yes, Mr. Chapin. Good morning, good morning. Nice to hear from you. How *are* you this fine morning?"

"Any word?"

"Oh no, not yet. Too soon for that. But they'll turn up somewhere, Mr. Chapin, they always do. You'll notify the hospital if you hear of their whereabouts, won't you, Mr. Chapin?"

"I have a feeling we should hold off a while on telling the police," I said.

"Oh yes, yes, yes. That's right. Shouldn't put out a bulletin yet. It goes over the state wire, you know. It can be awkward and troublesome if the police have to bring them back. Much better to persuade them to return on their own if we can. We always wait for at least a week before we phone the police. Unless of course they're dangerous."

He chuckled, for reasons that were wholly obscure to me. I urged him not to hesitate to phone me at any time, and then I tried to be a reporter for the San Francisco *Chronicle*.

My city editor, Abe Mellinkoff, was aware of what had happened (I had phoned him the night before), and was most understanding. He quietly told me I didn't have to work; but when I said I would rather, he was sensitive enough to keep me as busy as possible.

Twice a day for eight days I talked to the hospital, and for eight days there was nothing, absolutely nothing. Mark was in the void. O'Hara's anxiety rose like the mercury of a thermometer thrust into hot water. She didn't cry anymore, but neither did she sleep. We waited, and waited.

We began to think we had to notify the police, we just couldn't go on like this. But we wanted the hospital to take the initiative—they were the professionals, they had previous experience in handling hospital escapes. Why should the burden fall on us, just because we were the parents? The hospital wouldn't act without my recommendation.

It rained heavily, and we pictured Mark down with pneumonia in a country barn or in a Haight-Ashbury pad.

On the ninth day Mark surfaced. Late at night he appeared at the house in Fairfax where Pennell lived with Sara Howard and Vickie Barnes. It was where he had stayed with Pennell for a few days in the fall, and somehow, despite the crazy visions that swirled in his head, he had been able to find it. It must have been quite an effort.

Pennell, talking to us by phone in the morning, said he was "pretty bad"—filthy and undernourished. They fed him and gave him cigarettes. He had this fixed thought in his unpredictable mind. he wanted to live with Pennell and her friends even though it hadn't worked before, and he wanted to "go to school" at the College of Marin. Both of these desires were unattainable.

We asked Pennell if Mark would let us visit him in Fairfax. No, he would not. Would he talk to us on the telephone? No, he would not. After all, we had stuck him in a mental hospital and were bent on putting him back there.

I phoned the hospital's spokesman, who was his usual bubbly self.

"I told you he'd turn up, Mr. Chapin. Now if I were you, I'd persuade him to let you drive him back here. It's a bit frightening for the police to pick him up, you know."

How could we persuade him if he wouldn't even talk to us?

We were fearful that if we pushed too hard, he would panic and leave the Fairfax house. Pennell kept us in

touch. She said he sat in the living room for hours on
end, smoking and staring at the floor, and he trembled a
lot. She didn't know what to do with him, yet she couldn't
throw him out; she couldn't face that. Finally Mark agreed
to see us if we promised not to take him back to the
hospital. We promised.

He looked awful. His cheeks were flushed bright red
and his hair was matted. His feet were blistered and
crusted with dirt. He hadn't had a bath in almost two
weeks and refused to take one. He wouldn't meet our
eyes. We tried to find out where he had been, and he
didn't know, or said he didn't know. Had he taken any
drugs? He didn't know. Where was Steve now? He didn't
know.

We talked *at* Mark, not with him, as calmly and quietly
as we could. The hospital was where he should be, he
needed medical care for both his body and his mind, and
would he *please* let us drive him to Napa? He kept shaking his head, and trembling. He kept putting his right
hand over his heart. We left the house in Fairfax.

Nothing changed for five days. Pennell and Sara
Howard nursed him as best they could. On a Saturday
afternoon I informed the hospital that we had failed, that
Mark was in danger of exposure to more drugs, and that
we authorized use of the police.

"Fine, Mr. Chapin," said the jolly man at the hospital.
"I'll take care of that right away."

O'Hara and I went to a dinner party in Mill Valley
that night. We were among close friends, and we reck-
oned that being with friends, talking to them, drinking
with them, we would be subject to less strain than if we
were sitting at home while a Napa State Hospital escape bulletin was being put out on the police teletype,
with an immediate radio alert to every patrol car in the
state of California.

It was still a strain, however, so I drank quickly and
too much, for anesthesis. At ten o'clock our hostess said
we were wanted on the phone. It was Pennell. O'Hara

took the call, and I listened in on an extension. I was too muddled-headed to follow the details of Pennell's report, but it did get through to me that the police had come to the Fairfax house, than they had apprehended Mark, and that it had been very messy. That was the part I could comprehend despite my drunkenness: it was messy.

We left for home, O'Hara driving. I passed out on the living room couch.

I was still drunk when I woke, fully clothed except for coat and tie. I hadn't even taken off my shoes. I had an overwhelming sense of doom, a sense that if there were any remaining ties between Mark and me, they had been snapped by the events of last night. I had now directly authorized the use of police to hunt down my son. I was Judas.

The house was very still. I got up from the couch and walked out into the beautiful morning sunlight, the early sunlight, and started down the gradual slope toward the Sausalito waterfront, and I cried again. I couldn't hold it back. I guess I didn't want to hold it back. I had never felt such grief. There was a time, in 1945, when I suddenly realized I was never going to see my kid brother again, because he had been killed in World War II; but this was worse, because I was never going to see my son again.

I stumbled along the Sausalito waterfront, past all the boats rocking quietly in their moorings. I didn't want anyone to see me, I wanted to be alone with my grief. I mourned for Mark, and I mourned for the war, for all the wars, and I mourned for myself and my chopped-off leg, and I mourned for Pennell and how much, at the age of twenty-one, it must have hurt her to have the cops come and get her kid brother.

I walked on. Once a car slowed and the driver, whom I knew slightly, looked at me inquiringly, as if to offer a ride. I turned my wet face away from him and kept going. I walked for more than an hour, I think, and then I went home. I opened the bedroom door and O'Hara, waking, sat up in bed. "I can't seem to stop crying," I

said, and O'Hara lifted up her arms and I went to her and
she held me. She didn't say anything, she just held me,
and I said, over and over again, "My boy, my poor boy,
oh my poor boy." And finally I said "You know, the worst
part of it is he may be crazy but he's not as crazy as most
of the people on the outside." And in a paradoxical way, I
believed that. True, Mark couldn't cope with the world, but
often the world seemed so crazy as to be not worth coping
with. The world was torn by war and greed and racial
hatred. Mark refused to have anything to do with war,
and if he had only one cigarette he would share it, and
he did not judge a person by the color of his skin.

I stopped crying at last. O'Hara pulled off my clothes
and I got under the covers and slept.

The next day Pennell drove with me to Napa State
Hospital. She told me the whole story.

"It was wild," she said. "Jesus, what a night!

"They came about nine o'clock; there were two of
them, Fairfax cops, and except for one thing they were
pretty good about it. Mark was in Sara's room talking with
her when one of the cops knocked on the door and asked
if Mark Chapin was there. And like I was ready to flip,
'cause we had some grass in the house and I didn't know
if they would search us or not. God, it was crazy.

"The cop didn't seem angry or excited or anything. I
guess the other one was sitting in the patrol car; I could
see the car's lights. I said, 'Just a minute,' and ran into
Sara's room and said, 'The cops are here.'

"Mark didn't say a word; he jumped out the window.
Just like that, he jumped right out the window. It was
a good long drop to the ground, and in the dark and all;
but we could hear him scuffling around out there so we
figured he was all right. I ran into my own bedroom
where I can see the hill in back of the house, and from
there I saw Mark climb into this kind of weird treehouse
somebody had built out there.

"I just stood in my bedroom for a few seconds, like

I didn't know what to do; but then Sara all of a sudden freaked out, got really hysterical. She ran out the front door right past the cop and started screaming and crying, and the other cop jumped out of the car, and this is where the *first* cop really blew it. He ran down the stairs and pulled out his gun and waved it at Sara, kind of—all this mostly in the dark, except the cops both had flashlights—and there was Sara screaming her head off, and the cops yelling at her to shut up, and the neighbors beginning to come out of their houses to see what the hell was going on.

"Maybe the cop was inexperienced or something, and didn't know what Sara was going to do, but a *gun. Jesus.* I mean it was pretty far-out, with Sara so tiny and these two great big cops, one of them waving a gun.

"Mark must have heard all the noise, I mean he couldn't have missed it, because we all went back into the house, cops and all, and there was Mark. They asked him if he was Mark Chapin and he said yes, and by that time he was cool. I was surprised. Really, he was a lot calmer than Sara.

"They let Sara and me ride with Mark in the patrol car to San Rafael and then they turned him over to the sheriff's department and put him in a small room by himself. I think it helped him to have us along. And another good thing, the ambulance they sent down from Napa had Pedro—you know, the technician Mark says is a good guy—and Pedro rode with him back to the hospital.

"Incidentally, Sara really digs Mark. She wants to visit him as soon as she can."

That was the end of Pennell's story, and soon after that we arrived at the hospital. Mark was lying on his bed, limp and exhausted. He was awake, but probably under heavy sedation.

I sat down at the foot of the bed. "Hello, Mark, how are you?"

"Would you mind not sitting on my bed?" he said.

Chapter 15

MARK'S ESCAPE from Napa State Hospital established the pattern of his life for the next two years. And dreary years they were, too.

At Napa, in Ward Q-7, Mark shared a dormitory with forty males of various ages. The ward, decorated in pale, institutional green, was sparsely furnished. In addition to the beds, it had a ping-pong table, a pool table, a broken couch, and some folding chairs. The pictures on the walls had been drawn or painted by patients; they were expressions of violence or the fear of violence, done in vivid colors. Planes dropped bombs on people, and blood was let.

Opposite Mark's dormitory was a similar women's dormitory, and between them was a day room dominated by a never-silent television set. The nearby medical and records office was a glass-enclosed island; it made me think of a command post. The patients had access to a high-walled yard where Mark, O'Hara, and I occasionally held "picnics."

The ward psychiatrist behaved as if he suffered from chronic fatigue. Perhaps he did. He told us, during our single conference with him, that Mark was schizophrenic. It was the first time we had heard the word used to describe our son. OK, so he's "schizophrenic." Now what do we do?

Mark, like most of the patients, if not all, received regular doses of medicine. Drug therapy is the most prevalent therapy in state medical hospitals, for the obvious reason that it is the easiest to administer. Mark received suppressants, tranquilizers, Stelazine, Artane, things that would make him sleep, things that would turn him into a vegetable. And he did sleep; he spent most of the day on his untidy bed. He also attended group therapy sessions where, according to the therapist, he dozed. I used some *Chronicle* influence to get an interview with Dr. Robert Spratt, the hospital superintendent, and this led to an attempt at individual therapy; but Mark rejected it out of hand because he didn't like the psychiatrist. "That guy treated me like an animal."

Nothing much happened at Napa, except that Mark was forcibly prevented from taking narcotics (usually), and this alone was enough to bring some improvement: he became a little more aware of the world beyond his interior world. He continued to try to escape. He could only go outside in the company of an attendant. O'Hara and I visited him every week, delivering to him cartons of cigarettes and clean clothes and candy. He was extremely surly; after all, in his view we had cast him into a dungeon.

Mark may well have been the sloppiest and most disobedient patient on the ward—which did not endear him to the attendants, who, I felt, were generally decent people working at difficult, unrewarding jobs. So one day he was transferred to a much grimmer ward, where iron

WASTED WASTED

bars crisscrossed the windows and many patients never emerged from their catatonic trances. The transfer, I'm sure, was designed to frighten Mark, to show him what it was like to live with the real crazies instead of the temporary crazies. And it did frighten him; he became noticeably neater right way—he combed his hair—and pleaded with O'Hara and me to get him out of there. We told him that was up to his doctor.

In three weeks he was sent back to Ward Q-7. He brought with him a much better attitude toward himself and toward other people. There were glimmerings of self-respect.

Early in March he got his first overnight pass and we took him to Sausalito. It was good to have him free again, if only for a day. He stayed away from downtown, from "The Street," and he stayed away from drugs. But this small slice of freedom tired him, and he seemed almost anxious to return, Sunday afternoon, to the simple security of his bed in Ward Q-7.

He continued to get passes. Each weekend he was slightly better, more open, more revealing of himself.

In April he mentioned the big San Francisco peace march scheduled for the fifteenth.

"Are you and Mom going to it?"

"We sure are."

"Could I go with you?"

"Of course. We'd love to have you."

"That's great, That'll be out of sight."

A breakthrough, I thought; he was becoming a social being again. Ever since his first excursion into heavy drugs he had been contemptuous of marches, of rallies, of any community effort. He dismissed them all as futile.

But instead of breaking through, he panicked. Back in the hospital he must have wondered, with a growing anxiety, what it would be like to mingle with thousands of people, with all those strangers, and found he couldn't face up to them. At any rate, on April 12 the hospital notified us that Mark had escaped again. Over the wall and out.

O'Hara and I went to the peace march anyway, and it was a comfort.

In May, Mark appeared at the door. Of course he was ragged and dirty, he stank, he was as sick as he had ever been, and there was no doubt that he had used speed. He said he had lived in the Haight-Ashbury. Possibly; I'll never know. He said he didn't want to return to Napa, and Napa made no effort to get him. We let him sink back into his own bed in his own room. We felt helpless, paralyzed, utterly defeated.

And while he slept and was fed, a disturbing question flickered into my mind and out again: how did Mark support himself away from home? Was he no longer above a little male hustling, in time of need?

He stayed in bed, all night and most of the day, for a month. His brain was far off in the wild hazy distance.

By chance in Hanno's bar near the *Chronicle* building, I met a young psychologist from Huntsville, Alabama. His name was Alan Webb, he had a soft Southern drawl, he was active in the peace movement, he was staying in Big Sur on vacation, and I liked him immediately. He said, with no conceit and no false modesty, that he was a good therapist.

"What drugs has he used?" Alan asked.

"The usual. Pot, acid, speed. Mostly speed now. No heroin. At least, I don't think any heroin."

"What's happening to him now?"

"Nothing. Absolutely nothing. He stays in bed a lot."

"What do the doctors say about him?"

"They say he's schizophrenic."

"That there's a heavy word. Schizophrenic. A mighty heavy word to lay on a kid like that."

"Well, maybe he isn't. I don't know. I know he's very sick."

Alan Webb said he would very much like to talk to Mark, and I promised that if I could persuade him to travel I would bring him to Big Sur.

It was a struggle, but I got him to Big Sur.

"Are you a doctor?" he said to Alan Webb when they first met.

"I reckon so. Sort of a doctor."

"Are you crazy?"

"Don't know for sure. Don't think so. Are you?"

"No, I'm just part of the spirit world and I live in a tree trunk."

Alan took Mark for a walk in the Big Sur hills. They were gone for hours.

"He's mighty delusional," Alan said to me afterward, sitting on the fender of his brand-new Chevrolet truck. "He doesn't really know who he is. Some of the time he thinks he's Mick Jagger and some of the time he thinks he's Bob Dylan. Also, he's just a little bit effeminate. I think he's needed more authority."

"He used to complain bitterly that I spanked him too much when he was a child," I said.

"I've heard that so many times, with kids. So *many* times. What they usually mean is they *wanted* to be spanked, wanted some kind of contact."

In the end Alan recommended, in his soft slow voice, that I take Mark back to Napa State Hospital. There was no alternative, he said, and for Mark's purpose a state hospital was just as effective as a private one.

I took him back. He was so confused that he didn't resist. I had to get him formally readmitted. The admissions doctor was a senile clown who rambled on and on about Ivy League colleges and his acquaintances in the newspaper business in Washington, D.C. "What kind of reporting do you do, eh, Mr. Chapin?" It was agony listening to him. Why couldn't the old fart get *on* with it, get it over with?

This time Mark stayed in Napa for three months, escaped, came home, and was kicked out of the house.

Late one night a week after that O'Hara found him in
the garage, curled up in the back seat of her car.

"Can he come upstairs?" O'Hara asked me. "He says
he's got no place to go. He says he can't stop crying and
he's willing to try The Family at Mendocino State Hospital."

He came upstairs. He was loaded with speed. He told
us of a terrifying hallucination: he was lost in a forest,
he stopped and pissed against a tree, and what came out
was pure blood. He was pissing his lifeblood away.

But at least he was desperate enough to try Mendocino, and in the morning I got on the phone. I had to
obtain his discharge from Napa before Mendocino could
legally take him, and we felt threatened by bureaucratic
red tape but I got it done. And that afternoon I was in the
car again heading north with my sick kid beside me,
destination this time—The Family of Mendocino.

The Family was housed in an attractive one-story
building with a grassy interior courtyard and had a
campus appearance that was vastly different from Napa's
bleak, antiseptic façade. All of the patients were young
drug addicts. Most of the counselors were former addicts.

The psychiatrist who examined Mark said, "I've never
seen anybody quite so wired up. Look at him. Just *look* at
him, will you?" Mark was skittering around the courtyard
like perpetual motion. "We'll have to bring him down
first, with tranquilizers. That'll take a couple of weeks,
and then we'll see what we can do."

"Leave him alone for a while," the psychiatrist said.
"Don't you or Mrs. Chapin visit him for a month." That
was a relief. I wasn't going to have to see Mark for a
month.

Mark remained in The Family for three weeks and then
was transferred to Ward RT-1, where the program was
more in line with any other mental hospital program.
The Family people said, and I believed them, that Mark
did not possess enough self-discipline, nor was he tough

enough. He did not respond well to the harsh "rapping" that distinguished The Family encounter sessions.

But he did not seem unhappy in RT-1, he was not under lock and key, and he had a fine young psychiatrist, Dr. Calvin Janzen, who was in residence at the hospital. His main problem in RT-1 was a familiar but relatively minor one: his sloppiness. There were four patients to a room in RT-1, and Mark kept getting moved from room to room because his roommates complained. He spread ashes everywhere with his cigarettes, and he burned a saucer-size hole in his mattress.

O'Hara and I took turns driving up to see him—it was 240 miles round trip—and we worried about automobile accidents. The tendency was to drive much too fast.

We began taking him out of the hospital on weekends. I spent one night with him in a motel in Noyo, a raunchy little fishing town on the coast near Fort Bragg. We ate in an Italian restaurant. The waitress brought us two glasses with the bottle of red wine.

"I should tell you my son isn't twenty-one yet," I said.

"If it's all right with you, then it's all right with me," she said. "Rather have 'em drinking wine in here than out on the beach taking all kinds of dope."

"What," I said to myself, "if they do both?"

In the motel room after supper we slugged down a jug of cheap rosé, only Mark slugged down more of it than I did. I was amazed at how fast and compulsively he drank. It was as if any substance that would alter his consciousness, that would distort reality, was a good substance and had to be consumed right away. I heard him stirring around after I had snapped off the lights. He was fumbling for the wine jug in a corner of the room. "I'm quite a drinker," I thought, "but nothing like him." Of course that wasn't actually true.

O'Hara and I spent Christmas with him in a motel in Ukiah, five miles from the hospital. Again it was a sad Christmas. We had adjoining rooms. Mark walked into our room and promptly pissed on the toilet seat, as if to say, "You're not going to buy me off with a few lousy Christmas presents." I recall that in his room he raised the toilet seat.

We ate Christmas dinner in a restaurant that specialized in pancakes. It was called Sambo's. The turkey tasted like ashes.

In January, 1969, we made a start at family therapy with Dr. Janzen. Mark was unreceptive. He said he was fed up with Mendocino State Hospital; it wasn't helping him. Late in January the hospital called to say, rather casually, that Mark had walked out and was listed as AWOL.

"Ring us up if you should happen to see him, will you, Mr. Chapin? You can bring him back any time you want to, if he wants to come back. No problem."

I saw him the next day. He appeared to be in surprisingly good shape. He sat calmly in the living room and told us he had borrowed three dollars from another patient, hitchhiked to the Greyhound bus station in Ukiah, and bought a ticket to Sausalito. It was as easy as that, the way Mark described it—the act of a rational person.

He said he wanted to take make-up courses at the College of Marin so that he could get a high-school diploma, and then he would hunt for a job. He sounded as though he had planned his immediate future and had a fairly firm grip on it. O'Hara and I were very pleased. I said that first of all I would take him to a shopping center to outfit him with new clothes and shoes. Then, in a day or so, we would see about entrance exams at the College of Marin.

He was grateful, and as we left the house on our shopping tour, he said to me, "I'll be gentle with you guys. I really will."

Gentle with us. It revealed, I thought, an insight hitherto denied him.

I drove him to the College of Marin, where, despite his

nervousness, he got himself an examination schedule; and intermittently for the next ten days he took written exams. He started happily enough, but he couldn't handle the exams; they were too much for his fragile psyche, and I could see his confidence ebbing away.

His grades were disastrous. In two of the five tests he scored in the lowest percentile possible. His rank was one out of a hundred.

He celebrated the fact that he wasn't going to make it into the College of Marin by going downtown and taking on a heavy dose of speed.

Chapter 16

During our final session with Dr. Janzen at Mendocino State Hospital, the psychiatrist urged us not to discontinue family therapy. We had made no more than a start with Janzen and Mark was hardly cooperative. I did not think our prospects were good. But he was out of the hospital, sliding downhill again, and we couldn't simply watch and do nothing.

So I got on the telephone—I persisted in choosing doctors the way one chooses a gardener, by skimming the yellow pages—and called a Bay Area number and talked to another psychologist.

The "therapy" began at once. The psychologist, one of several who shared a large office, called me Bill and suggested that I call him by his first name, Marty. Marty said he and his colleagues didn't believe in last names: too cold, too distant. All right, Marty, I'm willing to go along with that. We're chums. Marty said he would be glad to see us—particularly glad, since he was eager to "get into" the problem of adolescent drug abuse in middle-class suburban society. "Who else but the Chapins?" I thought. Made to order for Marty.

At the designated time we dragged Mark to Marty's office and met our man. He had an iron grip, a hearty manner, and a strong voice. "Hi, Bill," he bellowed. He was "delighted" to see me, and O'Hara, and even delighted to see Mark, our sick son. And he was sincere in his delight, and in everything else. Marty was, as far as we got to know him, completely sincere, and so were the other psychologists we met in this place. It was palpable; sincerity came oozing out of them like toothpaste from a tube.

Our therapy room had couches, easy chairs, bookcases, and a few books. Like most therapy rooms, it was designed to make us feel relaxed and right at home. We settled down and tried to make ourselves comfortable, and the therapy began in earnest.

The emphasis was on our feelings: let them all hang out, give them free rein, don't be restrained. Don't rely on rational thought because that is emotionally constipating and therefore bad. We were expected to shout when we were mad, cry when we were sad, laugh when we were happy; and we were expected to do these things immediately, on that very first goddamn day. It was my sincere conviction that a few practical matters—such as a schedule, such as psychological tests for Mark—should be disposed of before we plunged headlong into therapy. When I tried to voice my convictions, Marty said, "You're thinking again. You see? You're *thinking.*"

During the first session Marty scored several minus points on O'Hara's score sheet. If he was really trying to get her mad, he succeeded. The trouble was that she stayed mad, and profoundly skeptical of Marty's understanding of the human beast.

"Do you and Bill have a good marriage?" he asked her.

"Yes, I think we have a good marriage. Like all couples, we've had a lot of stresses and strains—seems to

me anyone does in a world like this—but all in all, it's
been good. Yes, it's been good."

Marty hooked a thumb toward Mark. "Then how come
you got a kid like this?"

I could hear O'Hara suck in her breath. She gave a
long, careful, and rather icy answer. In sum, she said
our marriage could not entirely be blamed for Mark's
use of drugs and attendant illnesses. She said we had a
healthy, happy daughter.

Marty insisted we Chapins didn't look at each other
often enough, or ever touch each other. So we played
musical chairs, with the therapist's big booming voice
as the music, to rearrange the bodies.

"OK, Bill and Mark, you two look at each other. That's
right. No—no, no, no. Don't look away."

Silence. Mark and I stared at each other, like dumb
idiots.

"How do you feel? How does that make you *feel*?"

Mark said, "I dunno."

I said, "Just the way I felt five minutes ago. I don't
mind looking at Mark. I look at him lots of times."

Marty said, "Mark, I notice you never touch your
father. What's the matter? You afraid to touch him?"

"No."

"Then touch him."

Mark put a diffident finger on my arm.

"How does that feel? How do you *feel* touching your
father, Mark?"

"I dunno."

That's the way it went for an hour. What a farce.

And then, when the session ended and we shook
hands all around and got into the car, I asked Mark what
he thought of the doctor.

"I liked him."

"Did you really? How come?"

"He's the first one who took my side instead of my
parents' side."

I wasn't at all certain that Marty had taken Mark's

side, or anyone's side for that matter, but I didn't argue. It was unusual for Mark to be so forthright—"I liked him" —and I found that slightly hopeful. Even if I couldn't relate to Marty, maybe Mark could.

But next week, same time, same place, we didn't have Marty. We found he had assigned "John" to us as our regular therapist. John was less abrasive and less sure of himself than Marty, his boss, but he yielded nothing to anyone in the sincerity sweepstakes.

We began with a series of little question-and-answer tests.

"Mark, who do you think is the brightest member of your family?"

"Bill, who do *you* think is the brightest member of your family?"

"O'Hara, who do *you* think is the brightest member of your family?"

All three of us, in turn, said I was the brightest.

"Mark, how did that make you feel, when Bill said he was the brightest?"

"I dunno."

After the tests we had another round of touchie-feelies. O'Hara and I sat closely together, held hands, and looked into each other's eyes. They looked like the same nice old eyes to me.

John chided me once for holding back, for not using any four-letter words if those words were common in my vocabulary.

"Look," I said, "I can't act mad unless I *am* mad, and right now I'm not. Maybe a little irritated, that's all. And I can say 'fuck' and 'shit' in here if that's what you want me to do, but what's the point? I do know what the words mean, and as a matter of fact I use them quite often. Probably too often. But what's the point of using them in here?"

As we left the therapy room, John said, "Bill, I just

want to say you were great today. Just great. It was
beautiful."

I felt like telling him to go fuck himself; no doubt he
would have swooned with joy.

We had three more sessions. During the last one
Mark was stoned out of his skull, and admitted he had
smoked a joint just before we left the house. O'Hara and
I sensed that this new therapeutic relationship was soon
to be terminated. At the end of the hour John abruptly
announced that he had to go to Washington for three
weeks to attend a conference. I recalled Dr. William Soskin's similar announcement. "Why the hell are psychologists always flying off to Washington?" I thought. "And
is this their way of canceling out?" There was no logic
to this, but I was not in a mood for logic.

Mark was completely indifferent to John's absence.
He took to his bed. We existed. While we were existing,
Marty phoned to tell me of a very big deal. A famous
family therapist was going to give a couple of guest lectures to Marty and his crew, and perhaps the Chapins
would like to "sit in" as raw material.

I said we'd be there. Why not? Marty said, "Bring
your daughter too. She might enjoy it." Pennell agreed
to go with us.

Marty had exceeded himself in spreading the word.
Our therapy room was jammed with families who were
taking therapy. Babies were very much present. It was hot
and airless in the therapy room, and the babies cried.
Our guest lecturer was a woman, a very big woman,
straight out of a Wagner opera: six feet tall, bosomy, and
blonde. I thought, "Boy, I'll bet she's given hundreds of
couples the lowdown on how to improve their sex life,
and I'll bet she's a lousy lay—like going to bed with an
intellectual cow."

This large and ponderous woman sat down beside me
and started to talk. Her introductory remarks were not
unfamiliar: We, as families, *had* to have absolute free-

dom of speech; every human being, of every age, should feel free to say anything he wanted to say, at any time and at any place. She then turned to me with an inquiring face, and I gathered I was to exercise my freedom of speech.

"You mean that literally?" I asked.

"Oh yes. Of course. I have learned to say *anything* I want to say and I am *much* the happier for it."

"Well, I think that's a dangerous premise. What if I go up to a stranger on the street, a guy who's bigger than I am, and just because I feel like it I call him a motherfucker? I'm liable to get belted. And I think that would be dangerous. I mean, I wouldn't want to get belted."

She thought I had done wonderfully well. "There! You see? You said *exactly* what you wanted to say. Doesn't it make you feel better?"

And that's how it went. Other families were encouraged to vent their feelings without restraint, and some of them did. Mark, however, spent the entire hour pretending he wasn't even there. I discovered later that one of the persons in the room, an alcoholic, had been a patient with him at Napa State Hospital. It must have been very unpleasant for Mark; he somehow must have felt exposed.

Moments before we left the room, Pennell leaned over to me and whispered, "This is garbage."

I agreed.

O'Hara and I (Mark was missing somewhere, out on "The Street") saw Marty again. We told him Mark was much too sick to respond to this essentially casual therapy; it was a waste of time and energy, his and ours. He nodded. We said we had one final request: would he, as a psychologist, arrange for Mark to be given a series of thorough tests? We had hoped for tests all along. We were afraid that Mark's use of Methedrine might have caused brain damage, and we needed to know.

Marty said he could do this for us, and he did.

It took a week or so to set up the tests, which were administered by Dr. Lawrence Katz, a San Francisco clinical psychologist. Meanwhile, O'Hara and I indulged ourselves in an act of total desperation. We have tried everything, we reasoned. Mark won't stay in a hospital and he won't stay at home. When he is at home the emotional damage is enormous. He won't take private therapy; he won't stop taking drugs; he can't support himself. Why not cut him loose again, only this time cut him loose in another country so he won't be able to crawl home and stand, covered with shit, in the doorway of our home? Why not send him to England, the source of his useless dreams, the source of Mick Jagger and the rest of his heroes?

"Mark, we're going to give you a trip to England. It's what you've always wanted. When you're there, you'll be on your own. We'll see to it you have enough money to live on. You won't have to work. And perhaps, if you stop taking drugs, you can find yourself there."

He said a trip to England would be cool. He didn't jump with joy, but the idea kindled a few dormant energies, renewed a few old hopes.

The prospect nevertheless frightened him, especially as it got closer. He couldn't back out—too often he had appealed to us in past years to send him to England—but even he could recognize that the mechanics of the trip and the problem of living abroad by himself were beyond his scope. So here he was again, manipulated by parents who wanted to get rid of him. One evening I noticed him awkwardly thumbing through some papers on which, in his tortured handwriting, he had put down what could be interpreted as rules and maxims for living in England. Now and then his lips would move. He was studying the rules, trying to lodge them in his flawed memory. It was so sad to watch him, so pathetic, I felt so sorry for him. A crazy kid being sent into exile by his Mommy and Daddy. Yet I did not halt the process.

I got him his medical shots. I got him a round-trip

ticket on a freighter from San Francisco to London. I
drilled him on how to use traveler's checks. I arranged to
send money in small batches to the American Express
office in London. I made and gave to him ten Xerox
copies of his birth certificate. I took him to the San
Francisco passport office and filled out the application
form. The passport clerk asked in a tired, automatic
voice if all the statements on the form were true.

"Probably," Mark said.

"Yes, they're true," I said quickly, fending off the
clerk's sudden glance of suspicion: was this a smart-ass
kid putting him on? We got the passport.

Two weeks prior to Mark's departure date in April,
Marty phoned. He had the results of the clinical tests.
He was not allowed to give us the verbatim report, but if
we came to his office he would interpret it for us.

We went to Marty's office. He said that Mark had not
been cooperative during the tests and had not even com-
pleted them. Despite this, Marty said, the tests indicated
strongly that there was brain damage. He wanted to make
it as graphic as possible, put it into terms a layman could
understand. It was, he said, as if someone had taken a
revolver and shot a bullet through Mark's brain. The cells
carried away by the bullet would never be recovered.

Marty said he was sorry.

A few days later I got a bill from Dr. Katz, who did the
testing, for eighty-five dollars.

The testing and the subsequent report had one bene-
ficial effect: they impressed O'Hara and me with the utter
folly of trying to send Mark to England alone. He didn't
have the slightest chance of getting past the immigration
and customs officers in England even if he made it there
on the boat.

We told Mark that his psychological tests were dis-
couraging. We didn't use the words "brain damage." We
said he couldn't go to England. We said we were sorry.

"You guys," Mark said. "You guys always promise me
things and then take them back."

Chapter 17

WE ACCEPTED the Katz report with our minds but not with our hearts, and our sorrow brought us closer to Mark. The impulse was to treat him like a baby, to insulate him from the world outside our home. The prospect was to do this for the rest of our lives. What other prospect when a bullet, according to Marty, had removed part of his brain?

The days passed, one much like the next. Mark slept, ate, slept, ate. He was fairly amiable. The knowledge that he was not going to England may have been a relief to him, after his initial disappointment. O'Hara began to serve his meals upstairs on a tray so we wouldn't have to watch while he slobbered his food.

Early in May O'Hara happened to talk to Eleanor Haas, a pretty divorcée employed as a girl-friday by Dr. Harry A. Wilmer, a psychiatrist at Langley Porter Neuropsychiatric Institute. "You've got to see Harry," said Eleanor. "If anyone can help you, he can." And then later,

"I called Harry and he's very much interested. He wants to see you both. You're all set."

I had read about Dr. Harry Wilmer in the *Chronicle*. He was an innovator. His approach was not unlike that of the Mendocino Family: let the hippie addicts run their own society, right there in the hospital ward, and follow the slogan of The Family, that "pity kills." We went to Wilmer's office, which was dimly lit and contained a shiny black plastic pneumatic chair that no one sat in. He was a large man, slow-moving, bearded, with wrinkled clothes.

"Eleanor said you wanted to see me," he began, and waited. I had understood it to be the other way around, sort of. I told him I would give him the complete story, suggesting that he interrupt whenever he felt like it. And I thought, "God, I have said these words so many times to so many listeners. And all to no avail. I am sick to death of these same futile words."

When I finished, Dr. Wilmer pondered, rubbing his beard. In the soft light he was a Santa Claus in a messy blue blazer. He said, "Brain damage. I'm not so sure. It's very difficult to tell. I knew a kid I could have *guaranteed* would never come back, was going to be a vegetable, but he came back. Somehow. Began to lead an active life again, got a job. I think there may be a regenerative process, despite what they all say."

He stood up, walked to his desk, and absently rustled some papers. "Has Mark had neurological testing?"

"Just the psychological testing. At least recently. But we want neurological too. We've been trying to get that done."

"We can get that done here at UC. I'll make an appointment for you. And I'd like to talk to Mark himself. Bring him in, will you?"

Then, as we were leaving, Dr. Wilmer said, "You shouldn't feel so guilty. You mentioned when you got the police to pick him up and take him back to Napa it was the worst day of your life. But obviously you were doing

the right thing. It was the only thing you *could* do."
Kind words but small comfort.

I brought Mark in to see Dr. Wilmer. They were alone
for twenty minutes while I sat in a desk chair in the corridor feeling conspicuous. Then the doctor opened his
office door and silently motioned me inside. Mark was
slouched in a corner in the semi-darkness, with cigarette
ashes on his clothes.

"Mark and I are having a little trouble communicat-
ing," Dr. Wilmer said. "I'm not sure I know what he
wants. I'm not even sure Mark wants to get well."

My opinion of Dr. Harry A. Wilmer rose. He had only
seen my son for twenty minutes, yet he recognized the
root of the problem. Mark didn't want to get well. Months
later, Mark said the same thing in different words: "I
don't grow up. I stay a boy." Mark was off to the side
when he said that, looking at himself. It was like a com-
plaint about a plant that doesn't respond to food and
water.

"Would you consider going into Langley Porter?" Dr.
Wilmer asked Mark.

"How long?"

"I can't answer that. It might be several months,
might be three weeks, might be a day if you decided to
take off. Nobody would keep you there against your will."

"OK, I suppose so," Mark said. I was astonished. What
changed his mind about hospitals? Was there something
in Harry Wilmer he found he could trust? Or was he too
low to put up any more resistance? He turned to me and
said, in a suddenly firmer voice, "What about visits?"

"O'Hara and I would visit you as often as we could.
A lot more than at Mendocino, because it's a lot faster to
run in to San Francisco."

"Every *day*. You promise?"

"No, not every day," I said. His insistence puzzled me.
"All I can promise is that we'll visit as often as we can,
and it would probably be four or five times a week."

"OK," Mark said. "I'll go. You gotta match?"

Going home, I praised Mark for consenting to Langley Porter, and I praised the hospital. I laid it on thick, perhaps too thick. Dr. Wilmer had warned that admission to Langley Porter would take time; we would have to wait for a bed. It was a warning that proved painfully true. Twice a week I called the hospital; twice a week they said not yet, not yet.

Meanwhile, Mark and I followed up on the neurological appointment Dr. Wilmer had made. We saw one of the top neurologists at the University of California Medical Center, a gray eminence in a white smock sitting at a clean desk in a room devoid of warmth. He opened the nice clean folder handed to him by his secretary, said, "What's the boy's full name?" and wrote "Mark O'Hara Chapin" at the top of a blank sheet of paper.

"Now then," he said, "what's the problem?"

"Didn't Dr. Wilmer say anything about it?"

"No. No, he didn't, Mr. Chapin. You see, we didn't talk personally. His secretary and my secretary made the appointment."

"Well, I'd better tell you the whole story then."

The neurologist nodded approvingly, and I launched into it. He was the kind of person who verbalizes the notes he puts down on paper.

Me: "It's pretty hard to say for sure, but Mark has probably had between fifty and a hundred LSD trips."

The doctor, writing: "Has—consumed—an indeterminate quantity—of LSD. Yes, go on."

It was impossible not to allude to the Katz report. "Psychological—tests—indicate—brain damage." We talked about Mark, in his presence, as though he were a specimen in a bottle. It was cruel and humiliating— that is, if Mark comprehended.

Fifty minutes of the hour were consumed by my recitation of Mark's family and medical history. In the final ten minutes the doctor tested Mark's reflexes. He tapped his knees with a rubber hammer and made him

walk a straight line. He shone a light in his eyes. Once he
remarked that Mark displayed a little more strength in his
right arm than in his left arm. "But, of course, he's right-
handed, isn't he?"

I confirmed the accuracy of this observation.

Mark did not like to be touched by this man. At one
point he said, "I don't think you're a human being," which
amused the doctor.

It wasn't a bad judgment for a crazy kid, I thought.

When the tests were finished, I said, "What about the
EEG?"

"Oh, you wanted an EEG too?"

"Yes, please. We want as thorough testing as we can
get."

"Well, we'll have to schedule that. Talk to my secretary on your way out, will you, Mr. Chapin?"

We went home. I moaned and groaned to O'Hara that
doctors were worse than most people in regard to com-
munication.

I took Mark in for his electroencephalogram, which
he hated; a week later I was back in the neurologist's
office to get the results.

The doctor commenced with an "interpretation" of
the Katz report, a copy of which he had received. I reminded him that I had already been briefed on the Katz
report. He apologized and turned to his own material,
which was skimpy. He said Mark's responses to the reflex
testing were "flat," but there was nothing that pointed
specifically to brain damage.

"What did the EEG show?" I asked.

He had neglected to get the EEG results, which to me
were paramount. He phoned, and made a couple of
scratchy hieroglyphics on Mark's chart. The EEG hadn't
revealed much either.

"What's the conclusion then?"

"I would say, Mr. Chapin, that we cannot rule out the
possibility of minor, generalized brain damage, though
we cannot say for a certainty that he *does* have damage.

What we *can* rule out, pretty definitely, is the existence of massive damage to a specific area of the brain. None of the responses, either reflexive or EEG, indicate localized damage." I thanked him and left. He sure could talk without saying anything. He would have made a hell of a politician. He sent me a stiff bill, and so did the EEG lab, and so did Dr. Wilmer.

On May 27, Mark was admitted to Langley Porter Neuropsychiatric Institute. The long wait had put us all on edge, and O'Hara accompanied us in the car so she could help if he decided to run off. But he didn't. We got him inside. He was to be in Ward A–2, which was adjacent to Dr. Wilmer's hippie ward. His psychiatrist was to be Dr. David Leof, a tweedy, bearded, pipe-smoking man with a Phi Beta Kappa key dangling from a vest pocket. (Eleanor Haas, pleased that Mark had been assigned to Dr. Leof, said that one day he would be known as "super-shrink.")

During the admission interview Dr. Leof made two things plain: (1) he had attended Yale University, and (2) he was not afraid of vulgar language, "bullshit" being his reply to several of Mark's non-statements. He asked Mark to repeat sequences of numbers forward and backward. Mark was unable to do it. I was glad that Dr. Leof didn't ask Mark's father to repeat sequences of numbers forward and backward.

Mark was given a bed. Dr. Leof informed us that the first three weeks would be devoted to "evaluation," and during that period Mark's medication would be kept to a minimum. That made sense. They wanted to scrutinize the "normal" crazy Mark, not the doped-up crazy Mark.

During the three weeks we visited Mark almost every day. Then we were called back to Dr. Leof's little office. The doctor hedged a bit at first, and I don't blame him, considering what he had to tell us.

He said that Mark had been subjected to the most exhaustive and sophisticated testing available, he had

been examined by "everybody in the place, believe me."
He said it was impossible to escape the conclusion that
Mark suffered from chronic brain damage. He said Mark
had "moments of lucidity," and that during these
moments he could recognize his plight, his inability to
think; and this recognition so frightened him that he retreated into a hallucinatory state. He said we had to start
thinking not in terms of recovery, but in terms of custodial care; we should realize that Mark would never
marry, never have children, never hold a real job. He said
Langley Porter was not equipped to cope with Mark's type
of problem, but that the institute might be able to raise
Mark to a higher level of function than his present one.
He said he didn't know quite what to do about all this;
there weren't many places designed to handle Mark. He
gave us a magazine article about one possible place in
Vermont. He said he was sorry. He said we ought to at
least consider Napa State Hospital, on a more or less
permanent basis.

We said we would rather see Mark die on the street.
Dr. Leof said that was a terrible decision to have to make.
We agreed.

Finally, we reached a kind of entente. Dr. Leof would
keep Mark in Langley Porter and treat him as best he
could. O'Hara and I would go to England for three weeks,
partly to get away from the home scene, partly to see
whether England might offer a more congenial setting for
Mark, in an institution. We said he might be more "content" in England.

I saw Mark when we left Dr. Leof's office. He was in
the ward's medical records room; a woman was combing
his hair, trying to get the tangles out of it. He was peaceful, inattentive. He was "content," and it just about
busted me up to look at him. I had to get out of there in
a hurry.

Our passports were in order, and on June 20 we were
on a BOAC plane bound for London. We were to stay
with my sister Janet, who had married an English

architect and who hadn't seen O'Hara or me for years. We carried two medical reports. One, by Dr. Leof, described Mark's drug history and concluded, "Our diagnostic impression, then, is Chronic Brain Syndrome, secondary to psychotometic amphetamine and other long-term drug abuse." The second, by Dr. Edward Gould, Langley Porter's senior staff psychologist, described Mark's limited response to testing and concluded, "Mark Chapin's test protocols clearly indicate that he is suffering from serious brain damage, probably due to his orgy of drug usage over the past three years. The extent of his attempts to cover up his deficit makes it difficult to truly assess the degree of damage, or provide a clear picture of characterological factors and premorbid personality functioning."

We also had several names provided by Dr. Leof— the Tavistock Clinic, Maudsley Hospital—places where we could begin our inquiries. Dr. Leof mentioned that he was going to study at Maudsley in the fall.

We were met at Heathrow Airport by Janet and her husband Roger, a towering, upper-class, delightful, and totally absent-minded Englishman. It was dusk when we drove through London to their home in Highgate, and the city was beautiful—very green and beautiful.

For the first week we did nothing but unwind, and then we tackled Maudsley Hospital. It was not encouraging. Whenever we used the word "drugs," the Maudsley people—doctors and nurses alike—reacted as if they had been struck by lightning. We tried to persuade them that brain damage, not drugs, was the core problem now. They were unconvinced. They were puzzled, too; why, they asked in their polite British manner, had we journeyed all the way from San Francisco to seek help for our drug-addicted son when San Francisco was much better equipped to give him that help? They had heard of the Haight-Ashbury. That's where it started, wasn't it?

We tried Tavistock Clinic. No go. We tried several private psychiatrists. No go. We tried a mental hospital in the country. Sympathetic, but no go. And drugs were not the only bugaboo. They were mildly suspicious of our motives: perhaps we were seeking to exploit the National Health Plan's cheap medicine.

Through Roger we got an interview with a case worker employed by the Mental After Care Association—a sweet, motherly woman named Mrs. E. D. A. Jeffreys. And here we received our first encouragement. The After Care Association operated fifteen "half-way houses," most of them strung along the southern coast of England. The houses were small, accommodating ten to fifteen patients, adequately staffed and, judging by photographs, extremely pleasant. They were homelike. Mrs. Jeffreys saw no obstacle to Mark's eventual admission to a half-way house, despite his former drug addiction, despite his alien status. We told Mrs. Jeffreys that when Mark was well enough to travel, she would hear from us again.

We made a few more inquiries; we went to Wimbledon to watch the tennis matches; we went to two marvelous plays; we shopped; we ate in four good restaurants and one bad one; and then we boarded our plane for San Francisco.

I called Langley Porter. There had been some changes. Dr. David Leof had been transferred to another unit of the hospital. His replacement was a psychiatrist-in-residency, Dr. Edward Henderson, who urged me to come in for a talk as soon as possible. I said, "OK, tomorrow."

Mark seemed the same. He had walked out of the hospital twice, I was told, and was "on restriction."

Dr. Henderson was black, or, to be more precise, a very pale chocolate, and had soft defenseless eyes; a mere baby, fresh out of medical school. At least that was my first impression of him. O'Hara and I sat down in his office and he said, "Did you find a place for Mark in England?"

I was flabbergasted. I explained that our trip was exploratory, that we hadn't dreamed of lining up a suitable place for Mark in so short a time. Dr. Henderson said there must have been a misunderstanding, and I said there sure as hell had been. Dr. Henderson disclosed that he had sent us a telegram, which apparently arrived at my sister's home just after we departed. The telegram said that Mark was due to be discharged from Langley Porter, and what progress had we made? I thought, "Jesus Christ, what's going on around here?" I knew nothing of a telegram or a deadline we had to meet.

We were joined in the conference by a woman named Ellie Gross, a social worker whom we had never seen before. It was immediately evident that she was in charge of Mark's case.

"We've had several staff meetings about Mark," Miss Gross said, "and it was decided that Langley Porter couldn't help him any more. It's not set up for custodial care. He should be discharged."

"OK, but where does he go next?"

"We don't know," Miss Gross said.

"Look, *you're* the ones who want to discharge him. Find a place. You can't just throw him out on the street."

"We can transfer him to Napa."

"No. Absolutely no."

"Maybe you could hire a practical nurse to take care of him at home."

"Miss Gross, you've got to be kidding."

Miss Gross shrugged her shoulders. Nobody said anything for a while, and then Miss Gross delivered her ultimatum: "We can give you a week, until July sixteenth, to find a place for him. But on July sixteenth he's going to be discharged."

"Well, I guess you have the right to discharge him, if that's your medical decision," I said. "But I have the right, as Mark's father, to disagree with you. And I may as well tell you I'm going to use every bit of influence I can muster to keep him in here. If you want to take that as a threat, so be it. But we've got to have more time."

With that lofty little speech the conference ended. I called Dr. Leof's home that night and pleaded with him to intercede. I said I was outraged. He said he would call me back. He never called me back, and I haven't talked to him since.

I had lunch the next day with Carolyn Anspacher, a prize-winning *Chronicle* reporter who had written a great many investigative stories on the State Department of Mental Hygiene and its various institutions. Since Langley Porter was associated with the University of California, it was a unit of the state system and, I hoped, therefore vulnerable. Carolyn Anspacher, when she got her dander up, was a formidable opponent; and as she listened to my account she got her dander up. She promised to pick up the phone as soon as she returned to the *Chronicle* office. I went home and said to O'Hara, "I think the shit's going to hit the fan."

By ten o'clock the next morning Dr. Henderson was on the phone. "Could you come in for another conference, right away?"

Dr. Henderson was alone this time, with no Miss Gross.

"We've decided to try something new with Mark," he said. "We had another staff meeting, and we're going to try treating Mark like he was a schizophrenic. With medication. If he improves, then fine, we will keep him on."

"I think that's great, Dr. Henderson. I'm very much relieved."

"I understand you were in touch with a friend of yours from the *Chronicle*. Miss . . . ."

"Miss Anspacher."

"That's it, Miss Anspacher. Well, I want you to know our staff decision had nothing to do with that."

"Of course not, Dr. Henderson."

"And another thing, Mr. Chapin. If you have any more problems, bring them straight to me. I'm in charge of Mark's case."

"I will, Dr. Henderson, I most certainly will."

We shook hands and I left. I had bought some time. Or rather, Carolyn Anspacher had. Bless her.

Chapter 18

D<small>R. HENDERSON</small> and Mark were in group therapy when O'Hara and I arrived for a 10 A.M. appointment, and the doctor's office door was locked, so we sat on Mark's bed, waiting. This was two weeks after Mark had been granted his reprieve. Langley Porter Institute is ordinarily cloaked in fog, but today was a nice day; the sun slanted through the Venetian blinds, warming the rumpled bed.

Mark had painted another face. The patients were encouraged to paint, to get it out in the open.

"He's gone backward, hasn't he?" O'Hara said.

The new face was pinned to a composition wallboard behind the bed, next to an earlier face. You could tell they had been painted by the same tremulous hand and had come from the same troubled mind, but they were different. The earlier face showed resolution and even a little hope. Its lines were fairly firm, the background light blue, the mouth turned up in a kind of broken smile. The new face, reflecting the artist's latest mood, was dark with anger and despair, the mouth a thin slash and the cheeks covered with restless vertical strokes of green and brown. They looked like infected wounds.

We studied the faces. Mark walked out of the therapy room, leaving his peers, and approached us. He was wearing the beltless blue jeans and stained sweatshirt he had worn all week. His fly was unbuttoned.

"Hello. I guess I'll go to Vermont. By December. I'm going to be out of here in December—maybe December."

He put a half-smoked cigarette in his mouth and said, "Gotta match?" I shook my head and he turned to O'Hara. "You gotta match?" Then he shuffled away, favoring us with one quick glance of hostility before rounding a corner of the room so that we couldn't answer in kind.

"The only reason he's on this Vermont thing right now," I said to O'Hara, "is because he saw a picture in that *Vermont Life* I brought him, and he liked it."

I got the magazine and showed her: a stream, a covered bridge, a small white farmhouse and a red barn, in Kodachrome, too perfect in its brilliance, but seductive. When Mark had first seen it as he thumbed the pages he had said, "That's an interesting picture. That's where I want to live."

Now he came back, with a cup of coffee, from the dining room. He put the coffee on top of a pile of papers on his nightstand, spilling it.

"I could get a job there. Farm, or on a garden. Gardening maybe. This place—I'm going in December."

He picked his nose and asked if I had a cigarette. When I said no, he pulled a tattered pack of Kents from his pocket. On the nearby chest of drawers was one of Mark's familiar signatures: a cigarette butt balanced on its filter tip, the tobacco ash curled and dead. He had been forbidden to smoke in the dormitory; it was like forbidding the moon to rise.

"Vermont's fine," O'Hara said. "But do you know what it's like in December?"

"Snow?"

"That's right, snow. And ice. And very cold."

"Mmm—that's true," Mark said, and shuffled off again, staring at us. We had said something he didn't like. We had sabotaged his dreams of Vermont. We were against him.

The therapy session ended and Dr. Henderson ushered us into his office. As always, he was neat and stylish: turtleneck sweater, mod jacket, and expensive brown boots that gleamed. His eyes were fluid, his face benign and uncommunicative.

Mark opened the door, without knocking, and came in. He didn't want to be with us, but neither did he want us talking about him behind his back. It was an awkward choice.

"Mark's been saying he'd like to go to Vermont," I said.

"Oh?" said Dr. Henderson. "You have friends there?"

"Mmm. That's true."

"What do you plan to do in Vermont?"

Mark gave the doctor a hate-stare.

"I told Mark he'd probably like Vermont," I said, "but first he's got to get well, and learn to do the little things."

"Like what?" Mark said.

"Like buttoning your fly."

Mark buttoned his fly and gave me a hate-stare.

"Remember what you told me last week," Dr. Henderson said to Mark. "You wanted to discard your hippie image and start talking about things directly instead of—instead of, like in riddles."

"Mmm. That's true."

"It doesn't look like it to me," Dr. Henderson said.

A patient from the women's section of the ward walked past the open door, a beautiful girl who wore mini-skirts and black net stockings. She was twirling a cap that O'Hara had bought for Mark on Carnaby Street in London. Mark stood up and followed her, twisting around to say, "You treat me like an animal."

In fifteen seconds he was with us again. He couldn't afford to let us say something bad in his absence.

"I don't treat you like an animal," Dr. Henderson said. "But if you want to discard your hippie image, like you said, then you've got to start combing your hair and wearing socks."

Mark's legs, between his jeans and the tops of his desert boots, were coated with dirt. The conversation, I felt, was going round and round in circles getting nowhere. I started another lap. "Do I treat you like an animal?"

"Sometimes."

"When? What do I do?"

"Mmm. I don't know."

"I think Mark's mad at me because yesterday I asked him to take off his boots," I said. "I wanted to buy him another pair and I needed them for the size."

"They're like moccasins," Mark said. "I've walked about three thousand miles in them." They were indeed like moccasins, molded to his unwashed and stinking feet, the laces knotted. He could slip in and out of them without bothering with the laces.

The skin under Mark's eyes was pinkish, flushed, unhealthy—half-dollars of feverish color. Was that caused by the medicine, I wondered, or was hatred coming out of his pores?

The conversation, dying, refused to go another circle. It died. I got up and left, thinking to give it a chance to revive. I ambled across the dormitory and traced the contours of a jagged hole in the glass wall of the medical records room. Richard, a patient whom I considered excessively gentle, had hurled a chair through the wall two days before. The hole was covered with cardboard and white adhesive tape. Richard was a manic-depressive. I had never seen the manic Richard.

I returned to Dr. Henderson's office, which was silent except for little squeaks when the doctor swiveled in his desk chair. His desk was bare except for a carefully folded brown-paper bag. His lunch, I presumed. If you were a young psychiatrist, you probably had to brown-bag it at first. Later came the big fees.

"There's a Taurus bull in here and that makes a difference with Buddha," Mark said abruptly.

"Who's the Taurus bull," Dr. Henderson asked, "me or your father?"

"I don't know," Mark said, then saw the mini-skirted girl again and departed. Dr. Henderson closed the door and locked it. He spread his legs, resting his clasped hands in his crotch.

"What do you think?" I asked.

"Not too good."

"Not as good as last week."

Dr. Henderson nodded. "That's what we feel too. Remember, I told you the usual thing with this medication is that he would reach a plateau. Maybe he'll go on, and maybe he'll just stay there. But the staff pretty much feels he's reached a plateau now. I was quite hopeful about Mark when we started the medication. He was talking really directly to me. You know—saying he wanted to get straighter and talking about where he could go, what he could do. Now I'm not so sure."

"He seems much more hostile," O'Hara said.

"He can't manage a double response," Dr. Henderson said. "He can't understand that you can love him and still get angry with him. With Mark it's got to be one or the other, not a double thing. So when you show anger that means, to him, you don't love him and so he just retreats into himself."

"Do you still think he has brain damage?" I asked.

"No. We don't. If he had brain damage the medication wouldn't do anything for him. And he has improved."

"It must be difficult with him splitting all the time," I said. Mark was constantly leaving, and returning in time for supper.

Dr. Henderson nodded.

"I'll be frank with you," I said. "I don't mean that I'm afraid you're going to push him out of here. Not any longer. But I really don't believe I'd have much of a defense if you did discharge him now, on account of his going AWOL so often."

"Well, at the last staff meeting we decided to try the drugs for two more weeks and see what happens. If he shows more progress, we'll stick with it. If he doesn't, I don't think there's much more we can do. He's on a very heavy dosage right now. Just about the maximum."

"Have you found out any more about those board-and-care places?" O'Hara asked. (At an earlier conference Dr. Henderson had mentioned that the state had contracts with owners of private homes where discharged mental patients could stay.)

"Yes, I know where there are some," Dr. Henderson said. "But I don't think Mark would be accepted, the way he is now. You have to have a part-time job, at least, or be aiming for school, or something like that."

"What's he like in group therapy?"

"Very intrusive. Very interruptive. He'll make some wild poetic comment, no connection with what we're talking about, like that Taurus bull thing; and when we say, 'What'd you mean by that, Mark?' he gets up and walks away."

Dr. Henderson asked me to check with Mendocino State Hospital to see whether its staff would readmit Mark if necessary. I said I would. We thanked him and left. We found Mark lying on his bed, picking out a tuneless tune on his untuned guitar—a guitar I had bought him the week before. The sounds, I suppose, had a beauty that only he could hear.

"Gotta cigarette?" he said, and stopped playing.

Andy Curry, a senior psychiatric social worker, appeared. Andy was very black, always smiling, jaunty, at ease with himself. A competent person, one of the best in the place, I thought.

"Hey, will you do me a favor?" he said to O'Hara and

me. "Get him a great big comb. I want him to comb his hair, man, so it looks like Tim Buckley or Bob Dylan. You can do that, can't you, man?"

"He's *got* a comb," I said, pointing to the nightstand.

"Well, *use* it, man," Andy said to Mark, not unkindly.

The flush under Mark's eyes seemed to spread and turn to a deeper red. Now he was angry at me, O'Hara, Dr. Henderson, Andy, the whole against-him world. He spun away from us, walked toward the lavatory, and shouted back at me, "I *thanked* you for the guitar, didn't I?"

"Yes, you did, Mark."

He shuffled back. "Why don't you two leave?" he said to O'Hara and me.

The ward was locked. Mark knocked on Dr. Henderson's door. "These people want to leave," he said, and Dr. Henderson let us out.

Two days later we drove up Parnassus Avenue toward Langley Porter to visit Mark again. I saw him on the sidewalk, head down, hands in pockets, shuffling.

"Jesus, there's Mark."

I slammed on the brakes and O'Hara got out and tried to talk to him. He ran, and ducked into the UC Medical Center's Student Union Building. We caught up with him outside the swimming pool in the basement.

"Come on, Mark, let's go back to the hospital. Come on, now."

"How's Pennell?" he said. "How come she got free of you two?" Then he walked back into the hospital, with O'Hara and me trailing behind.

Chapter 19

Mark continued to run away from Langley Porter whenever the mood seized him. He walked into Golden Gate Park; he ventured into the Haight-Ashbury, which was now more Hell's Angel than hippie, and was strongly frightened by it; and he almost certainly took drugs. He insisted his absences were authorized—"I was out on a one-day pass."

The days dragged on; I expected a discharge any moment, but after the commotion I had made before, I suppose the hospital was reluctant to act.

Late in August he struck O'Hara across the face when she told him she didn't think he was well enough to leave Langley Porter. Late in August, too, he struck Dr. Gould, the staff psychologist who had furnished us with a "brain damage" evaluation. Meeting Mark by chance on Parnassus Avenue in front of the hospital, Gould tried to persuade him to return to the ward. He knocked the doctor's glasses off. Dr. Henderson told me of the Gould incident.

On September 2 he was discharged "against medical advice." The term implies no difference of opinion between doctors and administrators. What it really says is that the hospital throws up its hands because the patient is impossible to deal with. Mark wasn't in Langley Porter when it happened. We didn't know where he was. Nobody knew where he was. Dr. Henderson called to say that as of this date Mark Chapin was no longer a patient at the Langley Porter Neuropsychiatric Institute. I had no rebuttal. I said thank you for calling, and goodby, and hung up.

The first word came in a week, from a young housewife who lived above the basement apartment occupied by the close friend of Mark's who had been busted with him in 1965 for being noisy and drinking wine in a car in San Rafael. The housewife called, asked if I had a son named Mark Chapin and, when I said yes, told me Mark had broken into the basement apartment. She said the tenant was in New York, and she had no idea when he would be back. She said she didn't think he would be pleased.

I went over immediately. The apartment was empty. Mark's guitar was on an unmade bed. Orange peels were on the floor. Papers covered with Mark's illegible handwriting were on the desk. He had been composing "poems." A gas burner was on, full on. Sooner or later he would burn himself up or blow himself up. I closed a valve in the gas line near the floor and hoped that Mark was too crazy to discover why the gas had failed him.

Mark was gone, but his sickness filled the apartment, and it made me feel awful to be there. I left as soon as I could.

Two days later a Langley Porter doctor phoned me shortly after supper. "Your son Mark is here, in the lobby. His story is pretty confusing, but he says he visited a swami in San Francisco and a couple of cops came to the swami's house and brought him here. He's not under arrest, but we can't readmit him, you know. We'll try to keep him here in the lobby if you want to come and get him."

I went and got him.

"Hello, Dad," he said. "I was out on a pass, but they won't let me back in."

"I know, Mark. I guess you'd better come home with me, don't you think?"

He went back to his upstairs bed again. There was no place else. The next day he said he was going downtown, and could he have a little money? And I, impulsively, pulled a ten-dollar bill out of my wallet. His eyes, those dead eyes, suddenly widened—it was the most money he had seen in years. He took the bill, thanked me, and left.

It was a destructive thing to do, giving him all that money, inviting him to buy drugs. It was an act of abandonment—here's your cash, get out of my life. O'Hara and I quarreled bitterly over the ten dollars and I got very drunk. In the morning, hung over and full of remorse, I cried.

He disappeared for five days. The next time I saw him he was sitting on the sidewalk near the water's edge in Sausalito with four other derelicts. They were drinking from a bottle wrapped in a newspaper. I stopped the car and called to Mark; he rose slowly, swayed, stood upright, and stumbled over to the car. He sort of fell into the back seat. He was wearing a ragged khaki greatcoat that reached his ankles (purchased with part of the ten dollars?) and he looked like an old, old man. He wasn't old; he was twenty.

One day during this chaotic and horrible month when he was in and out of the house, Mark proposed that he live in "the hippie commune in the Presbyterian Church." I doubted the existence of such a commune, and said so. He insisted. I said, "All right, let's take a look. Get in the car. You show it to me."

I was wrong. Not only was there a hippie commune in the basement of the church—with hippies lying on Army cots, hippies washing dishes, hippies listening to a hi-fi set—there was a sign on the door that said, "No dope, no pets inside."

I thought the place looked remarkably like the ward of a mental hospital.

Mark and I talked to a nameless, shirtless "leader." "Sure, he can stay here if he helps do the chores. But no dope, no *stash*, man; we been hassled by the cops lately and if they catch us with dope we're fucked. Maybe you could contribute a little bread for, you know, food?"

I said I would contribute. We drove back home, got Mark's meager belongings—clothes and the guitar—and returned. I gave ten dollars to the leader and promised ten dollars every week while Mark lived there. The hippies who clustered around us to witness the financial transaction were impressed. Here, in all likelihood, was the richest kid in the commune.

I said to O'Hara, "That's great. Maybe he'll stay there. He's with his own people."

He stayed in the Presbyterian Church for one day— which was two days less than O'Hara had predicted and many days less than I had hoped for.

He walked into the house and headed straight for the kitchen without saying hello. He opened the refrigerator to check the goodies. O'Hara was in the midst of cooking something difficult. José Miura, a Basque gardener who periodically worked for us, was with his son in the back yard, cutting down a big acacia tree. It was not a graceful time for Mark to return to the bosom of his family.

"What are you doing here?" I asked as he reached into the refrigerator. It was a hot day, but he was wearing the khaki greatcoat and a film of sweat covered his face. He smelled bad.

"Came up to get some food. Just came up for supper."

"Wait a minute, Mark. Hold off. Stay *out* of that refrigerator. What about the church? The idea was you were supposed to live there, and *eat* there. That's why I gave them ten dollars, to go into the kitchen fund."

The anger was building up inside me, anger I had never felt for him, to this degree, before. What *right* did he have to do this to us, to wreck our lives like this?

"They kicked me out," Mark said. He started to pace.

"Why?"

"I don't know." Pause. "I had a fight with them."

José Miura's chain saw, biting into the acacia, was making a terrible racket. It was hard to hear.

"But *why*?" I said. "I suppose you wouldn't do any of the chores?"

"Yeah. They copped."

"What do you mean, they copped?"

"I don't know. They didn't understand. You wouldn't understand."

He couldn't stay still. He started down the front stairs for no reason at all and then returned to the kitchen. I followed him from room to room.

"I've got a job," he said.

"Bullshit."

"I've got a job at the Spinnaker."

"Bullshit . . . you haven't got a job and you'll never have a job. You sure as hell couldn't get a job in a restaurant like the Spinnaker. You only lasted one *day* at the church, one single fucking day. OK, where you going to stay now?"

"Staying with Bill-if-you-forgive-me."

"Who's Bill-if-you-forgive-me?"

"Bill Blackmore—you know."

"Bullshit, Mark. He doesn't have a place to stay any more than you do."

"Mmm. That's true." He put his hand over his heart, an old gesture. "Just came up here for a loving visit."

"What about the ten dollars?" I said. "I suppose that's gone."

"They stole it."

"They couldn't *steal* it, Mark. I gave it to them for your share of the food expenses. That was the idea. Remember?"

"Mmm. Well, I'm doing OK. I'm sleeping with the chicks at Langley Porter. I'm studying Japanese."

"You're not in Langley Porter now, Mark," O'Hara said. We were now back in the kitchen.

"Mmm. Do you want to listen to me at my level? I mean, there are epochs on the mountains."

"We're listening," O'Hara said. "I don't understand you."

"Well, Don is faster than war."

"Who's Don?"

"My boy friend," is what I think he mumbled.

"I'll get you a plate of food," O'Hara said. "But first will you *please* take a shower so you don't smell up the whole house?"

He moved here and there like a waterbug, up the stairs, out the front door, and then he went to the bathroom and turned on the shower, full force. It ran for fifteen minutes while O'Hara and I took turns shouting at him not to use up all the hot water and not to flood the bathroom. He emerged in a cloud of steam, with nothing on but his pants. The rest of his clothes he left in a heap on the bathroom floor. O'Hara served him his food on a tray in the TV room, where he would not be seen by the Basque gardener and his son.

It seemed to take him hours to eat. I looked in on him and saw that between mouthfuls he was thumbing through the pages of a big expensive book about Japanese Noh theater.

"No, goddammit," I said. "Put that down. I don't want you dirtying that book with your greasy fingers. Put it down. And hurry up and finish your food and get out of here."

He stood up and headed for the back of the house, carrying a bowl of chocolate pudding. He was going to eat his dessert outside.

"Don't go out there," I said.

"Why not?"

"Because I say so," I said.

"We don't want those people out there to see you, the way you are," O'Hara said. "We're ashamed of you."

He turned to confront us both. "I'm going to psychologically kill you," he said.

He started out again, and then I was after him, out of control. He must have seen it in my face, he must have known that violence was upon him, for he shouted, "War —war—war." I swung as hard as I could, and even as I missed I thought, "That's lucky; if I had hit him there would be blood all over the place and he would be hurt, and he would plunge through the screen door into the back yard where José Miura would see him, and see the blood."

The chocolate pudding flew out of his hands and I heard the bowl hit the floor and break. I got an arm lock on his neck from behind, and Mark chanted, "War is hell, war is hell, war is hell, war is hell."

I wrestled him into the living room—he had no stamina and no strength, and it was easy. For one fleeting moment I thought, "We're both crazy and O'Hara ought to call the police." I threw him to the floor and straddled him, pinning his arms. He lay there panting.

His eyes were mad, but suddenly they filled with tears. I noticed a brown smear on his left shoulder and mistook it for blood. It was chocolate pudding. I said quietly, "You are not going to kill me psychologically and you are not going to kill me any other way because I am bigger than you and stronger than you. I know war is hell. I've seen a lot more war than you have. Sure, war is hell, but that doesn't give you the right to come into this house and refuse to do what I tell you to do."

"Will you let go my arms if I apologize?"

"You don't need to apologize. All you have to do is say you'll pay attention to me in this house."

"OK."

I let him go. He sat in a small alcove next to the fireplace. He was shaking like a person with malarial fever and rocking back and forth. I said, "Mark, oh Mark.

What's going to become of you? War is hell but it can't be any worse than your life right now. Your life must be *awful*."

Then, through his madness, he got a glimpse of himself; he had to admit that his life *was* awful, and it was more than he could bear. His grief and his pain came out of him in hoarse, racking sobs. He was hunched over, shaking terribly, his hands hidden in his lap. He was naked except for his dirty ragged pants, and it seemed to me that his lament was for all the naked, tortured, gentle, defenseless young people thrust against their will into a miserable world.

I slid in beside him, put an arm around his shoulders, and pulled him toward me. I was suddenly conscious of how many big red blotches there were on his back. It was years since I had seen him cry. He couldn't afford to cry.

"It's all right, Mark," I said. "It's all right. Let it all come out."

O'Hara put a hand on his face and said, "Oh, Mark, please let us get a little bit close to you. Just a little bit. Please."

He was a little quieter now. José Miura's chain saw was still rasping away in the back yard as he cut the tree into firewood. I said, "Mark, why don't you—I think the best thing for you is to go upstairs and go to bed."

I followed him upstairs. He started to get into bed just as he was, and I told him softly to take off his pants so he would be more comfortable. He did this, and as soon as his head was on the pillow and the covers were pulled up he expelled some more of his grief, sobbing and gasping, crying out that war is hell. I sat beside him.

"Mark, you've got to let us help you. You're very sick, you've got to realize that. And maybe when you do realize that, we can help you get well."

He turned away from me, toward the wall, and he said, without the least sign of confusion, "I won't get well until they stop the war in Vietnam."

He was sane, my son was sane, and everybody else was crazy.

I patted him on the shoulder, he was quiet for a while, and then he sat up. "Gotta cigarette?"

I got him one from a pack on his desk and he smoked. But he was moving back into his interior life, into the shelter of his madness, the only shelter he felt was available to him. "I'm happy," he said. "I'm intelligent. I'm more intelligent than you. I help people. I just talk to them down there, along the linear line, that is. Besides"—his fingers formed chords in the air—"I'm studying the guitar. Oh, and I'm studying Japanese and sleeping with the chicks at Langley Porter."

"I know, Mark. I know. That's right."

"I just came up here to communicate, like—on the line there's me [he traced an imaginary line on his blanket] and there's you."

"You mean we're on each side of the line, Mark?"

"Mmm. That's true."

"I think you ought to get some sleep," I said. "Would you like a tranquilizer?"

He said he would, and I got him one, which he swallowed passively. As I was leaving the room he said, "Can I sleep here tonight?"

"Of course."

For several minutes I heard him walking back and forth from his room to Pennell's room, and then he was quiet. I checked. He was in Pennell's bed, on his stomach, one arm hanging out, fingers on the floor. He was deep in sleep.

Early in the morning I heard the refrigerator door being opened and I got up. He had his pants on, and his desert boots, and a huge black silk kimono we had brought from Japan. His hands shook. "I'm going into San Francisco and find an apartment," he said.

"No, Mark, you're not. You can't find an apartment. And why are you wearing that kimono?"

"I found an apartment once before."

"When?"

"I was on a pass from Langley Porter."

"Where was it?"

"On Pierce Street."

"OK. Go ahead and try. But not in that kimono."

I persuaded him to wait until O'Hara could fix him breakfast. I told him he might have better luck looking for an apartment if he combed his hair, pulled up his pants, and wore some socks. He glared at me, then went upstairs and returned wearing socks.

"If I ever have a kid," he said, "I'm going to bring him up differently. Summerhill."

"That's a good idea."

He ate his breakfast, then headed for the front door.

"Can I have fifty cents?"

"No, Mark."

He went out. I said goodby, but he didn't answer me.

Chapter 20

O<small>N OCTOBER 2,</small> Mark and one of his friends were arrested in Sausalito. The Crime Report read as follows:

At approximately 2:15 P.M., reporting officer was detailed to 33 Miller Avenue regarding two suspects, possibly under the influence of narcotics, walking in the area. On arrival reporting officer observed the two suspects walking out the front gate of 33 Miller to Miller Avenue. Reporting officer approached suspects and immediately advised them of their rights per Miranda. Both suspects stated they understood their rights and they would talk to reporting officer. One suspect stated, slurring his words, that he was visiting friends, but he didn't know where they lived. The other suspect, also slurring his words, stated he wasn't high and nobody could prove it. Reporting officer observed that both suspects had pinpointed pupils. Both suspects, while talking to reporting officer, had a hard time standing on their feet. They would fall backwards, attempt to correct, then fall forwards. Reporting officer checked both suspects' heartbeat and the beat appeared to be faster than normal. Both suspects appeared to be very nervous with the bodies shaking considerably. After speaking with the suspects and observing their balance and coordination it was obvious to reporting officer that they were under the influence of narcotics, to such a degree, they were unable to care for themselves. At this time both suspects were placed under arrest for 647f PC, under the influence of narcotics. They were transported to the Sausalito Police Department, booked, then transported to Marin County Jail.

Mark and his friend spent two nights in jail before they made a phone call and were bailed out. Mark's first version of the arrest was that he was wholly innocent— the cops busted him just to be mean. Months later he changed this. He said it was all his friend's fault—"he gave me some speed, a big dose of speed, in his apartment."

The other boy, an exceptionally handsome and talented youth, had a history of drug-taking that compared with Mark's, I learned from his mother.

O'Hara and I engaged Barney Dreyfus, an attorney we had known socially for fifteen years, to represent Mark, and this set off a depressing series of conferences, phone calls, letters to and from doctors, and trips to court. Barney, throughout, showed enormous patience, skill, and sympathy. If it was Mark's design to convince Barney that he could beat the rap on the grounds of mental incompetence, he certainly succeeded. His remarks were wild. Barney, taking notes, asked him why he didn't phone his parents as soon as he was in jail, and Mark replied, "There were fifty monkeys at the airport, that's why."

Barney got the case continued to give himself time to round up medical support, and Mark, frightened by the arrest, stayed relatively close to home.

In the middle of October O'Hara went to Montreal to visit her ailing mother. She needed a break, too. I assured her that Mark and I would get along all right and pledged that, whatever the provocation, I would not fight with him. But with O'Hara gone, he was apprehensive. He always slept with his window wide open so he could escape if I were to threaten an attack. Once, when I was cleaning his room, I found a sharp steak knife half-hidden by the window sill, within easy reach when he was lying in bed. I returned it to the kitchen without telling Mark. The next day the knife was by the window sill again.

And I, in turn, always remembered to lock my bedroom door at night.

He broke the silence of one of our typically silent lunches one day to announce that he was going to the Mental Health Center at Marin General Hospital in San Rafael to "get a little therapy."

"That's fine. You go right ahead."

No chance of that happening, I thought. I was wrong. At 2 P.M. I got a call from Leonardo Marmol, a psychologist at the Center who had seen Mark briefly in 1967. "Know anything about Mark coming up here for treatment?" he asked. "He's here right now."

"What's he doing?"

"Sitting in Dr. Liikane's office. We're not really equipped to deal with him here, you know."

"See if you can hold him there and I'll be right up. Maybe the three of us could work something out."

I was there in twenty minutes, but Mark had left, apparently in a panic, when Dr. Juhan Liikane, a staff psychiatrist, started to question him about his arrest. I had two middle-of-the-lobby interviews, both unsatisfactory. In the first, Dr. Liikane chided me for getting a continuance of Mark's court case—"These delays just add to their tensions"—and then, "Who did you say your lawyer was?" In the second, Marmol suggested that I try to place Mark in a hippie commune. I told him that had already been tried and Marmol, concluding the interview, said, "I feel very impotent to help you."

I thanked Marmol and drove for an hour in the area surrounding the hospital, hunting for Mark. I didn't find him, and he failed to come home that night.

Three days later, on October 28 at 8 P.M., the phone

rang. "Will you accept a collect call from Mr. Ray Cosgrove in San Francisco?"

I started to say I didn't know any Ray Cosgrove when a rough, booming voice interrupted: "Hey Bill! It's Ray. You remember. The guy in Mark's ward at Langley Porter."

I did indeed remember. Ray was an alcoholic in his fifties. He had been kind and helpful to Mark, and I accepted the call.

"Hey Bill! Mark and I are in jail here, down at the Hall of Justice. Two-fifty bail each. If you come down with seventy bucks cash you can bail us both out. I can pay you back right away. No problem there."

"What's Mark charged with?"

"Oh, nothing much. He went to Langley Porter and tried to steal some pills. Something like that."

"And what about you, Ray?"

"I was over to Macy's and I tried to snitch a pint of brandy. They caught me. I've been here since last Friday. Mark only got here last night. Can you come down right away? Go to Puccinelli's bail bond office. They're old friends of mine."

I hung up, sighed, cursed, got in the car, stopped at The Bottle Shop in Sausalito to cash a seventy-dollar check, and drove to San Francisco's Hall of Justice, a pile of concrete as forbidding as the Bastille. Puccinelli's bail bondsman refused me. I went next door to Graf's, where I was accepted after the bail bondsman, a melancholy Chinese, phoned the *Chronicle* to verify my credentials.

I filled out long forms. One form stipulated that if Ray Cosgrove or Mark Chapin failed to appear in court at the proper time, I would have to pay the full bail. I signed the form.

Armed with the papers, Mr. Chun and I crossed the street and took an elevator to the jail on the eighth floor. Mr. Chun said the prisoners had to be released to his custody. A big steel door clanged open and shut, and we waited on a narrow wooden bench while a police officer carried out the procedure for springing Mark and Ray. While we waited, two massive cops in helmets and black boots brought in a muscular black youth whose hands were tightly handcuffed behind his naked back. "Mothuhfuckahs! You fuckin' mothuhfuckahs!" he screamed at the cops. They didn't mistreat him (at least in my presence); they didn't react at all. They had no regard for his humanity; he was just a chunk of black flesh to be rendered harmless and put behind bars. It would have been better if they had shouted back at him.

Mark and Ray stepped up to a counter, presumably to pick up their "valuables." Mark's raincoat was streaked with white paint. Ray had a week's growth of whiskers and his feet were in shabby slippers. He looked like a drunk. They came over and I shook hands with Ray. As an officer let us out of the jail Mark said, "I'm thinking of going up to Mendocino and getting my head straightened out."

Both of them asked for cigarettes, which I supplied. Ray was jaunty, full of little jokes. It was grotesque.

Back in the bail office, Mr. Chun instructed me to have Mark in court at ten o'clock the next morning. Ray, all hyped up, made several noisy and pointless phone calls and then said, "I don't feel like going to sleep now. Let's all go to Sausalito and grab a bite to eat. We can go to Zack's—Sam's an old friend of mine—or to the Alta Mira. I can stay overnight with Sam, or at your house if you have an extra bed."

It occurred to me that Ray's mind was just as unhinged as Mark's, only he was noisier. I told him I wanted to get Mark cleaned up and in bed, but I would be glad to drive him to his home. Ray didn't have a home. I drove him to a couple of flea-bitten hotels and to the Elks Club, all the while listening to his grandiose schemes for financial recovery. None of these places would let him in, and finally I dropped him off at a delicatessen.

"What happened this time?" I asked Mark when we were alone.

"It was an illegal arrest."

"They're always illegal arrests with you, Mark. But tell me about it anyway."

He said that after he left the Community Mental Health Center at Marin General he stayed two nights on Mount Tamalpais—"with some people, some hippies, I don't know who they were"—and he started to hallucinate badly. So he hitchhiked to Langley Porter, saw a doctor and a nurse, and then, on his way home, stopped to rest outside the Presidio, the big Army base in San Francisco.

"I was sitting on the wall there when the cops busted me. I wasn't doing anything at all. It was illegal."

"How did they treat you?"

"They treated me fine."

I got Mark home, cleaned up, fed, tranquilized, and into bed; then, with apologies, I got Barney Dreyfus out of bed. By now it was midnight. Barney said he would meet us in criminal court at the Hall of Justice at ten in the morning.

Trembling, picking his nose, smoking, waving to strangers as if to ward off loneliness, Mark appeared in court and got his second continuance. After his appearance, we sat on a bench in the hall and Barney read the arrest report. "The cops say they found a vial containing ninety-one blue pills in Mark's pocket. They say the prescription was made out to a Beverly Hansen, by a Dr. Kalin; but that name had been scratched out and 'Mark Chapin' written above it."

"Yeah, that's right," said Mark. "That's the doctor— Kalin."

"Who's Beverly Hansen?" Barney asked.

"She's the nurse I talked to."

Barney raised his eyebrows. "Well, we'll leave it at that for now," he said. "I'll see if I can talk to the cops."

Home again, angry, believing that Mark had stolen the pills and was lying, I phoned Langley Porter and asked for Dr. Kalin, spelled K-a-l-i-n.

"We have no Dr. Kalin here."

I relayed that information to Mark, who was upstairs lying on his bed.

"That's very strange," he said, and I agreed.

I then managed to reach Dr. Edward Henderson, who sounded cold and distant, as though he didn't want to be reintroduced to Mark's problems. He said he knew nothing of a visit to Langley Porter by Mark.

I relayed this to Mark also. With an unusual amount of strength in his voice he said, "Let me talk to him."

I dialed Langley Porter again and handed him the phone.

"Is Dr. *And*erson there?" A short wait, and then, "This is Mark Chapin. Who was that doctor you sent me to the other day?"

He picked up a pen while still holding the receiver and wrote "Richard Galin." A few minutes later I was talking to Dr. Richard S. Galin, a psychiatrist at Langley Porter.

"Yes, I did see Mark, day before yesterday. I was the doctor on call in the outpatient clinic. I wasn't familiar with his case but Dr. Anderson brought me his records. Mark complained of hallucinating, but it seemed to me as I talked to him that he was fairly intact, and I was impressed by his coming in to ask for help. Sometimes a person can get over a rough period with the help of tranquilizers, so I gave him the Stelazine."

"But the cops say he had ninety-one pills. Isn't that an awful lot to give to a patient at one time?"

"No, that's common enough practice, Mr. Chapin. At times we prescribe as many as two hundred. It's almost impossible to kill yourself with tranquilizers. The barbiturates, yes, but not tranquilizers."

Dr. Galin confirmed that he had scratched out a typewritten name and written Mark's name on the vial of pills. He said they were the only ones he had available in his office. He said, further, that he would be willing to testify in court about the episode. I thanked him, went upstairs, and apologized to Mark for casting so much doubt on his story.

"That's all right," he said.

"Do you want some Stelazine? I can get some for you if you like."

"I'll stick with what I've got." He had some Thorazine, which had been prescribed by our family general practitioner.

I relayed Dr. Galin's report to Barney Dreyfus.

"That's good," said Barney, "but there's one thing that bothers me. Apparently Mark told the police he was under the influence of narcotics, which is what they booked him on."

"I don't know what to make of that," I said.

"We'll have to wait and see what happens in court. I don't think we'll have too much trouble."

O'Hara was due back from Montreal on November 9. A few days before that I risked leaving Mark in the house while I did an errand. "I'll only be gone for twenty minutes, Mark. Please stay out of the kitchen."

He was standing in the middle of the living room when I returned, with an earthenware mug in his hand. "Can I have fifty cents to go downtown?" he asked, and I smelled the sharp smell of burned food. I ran into the kitchen. The stove was covered with scalded milk, the tiny apertures in the gas burners were clogged with milk, and a scorched saucepan was in the sink. It would take me hours to clean up and get the stove operating again.

"Mark, for Christ's sake! No, you can*not* have fifty cents. Why the fuck should I give you fifty cents? *Fuck you!*"

He jumped when I screamed at him and fled upstairs.

All day long I ragged him cruelly. When he was eating his TV supper, he mumbled some words.

"I can't understand you."

"That's because I'm speaking Japanese, or Chinese."

"You speak so many languages, it's unfortunate English isn't among them. Then maybe we could communicate better."

Washing the supper dishes, I discovered another scorched pot, under the sink. He had tried to hide it. I took it upstairs and tossed it at him. "Here, I suggest you keep this in your room as a reminder of what a mess you made in the kitchen."

He caught the pot as though it were still hot.

In the morning he was gone. I was still in bed when I heard the front door slam shut. I went up to his room. He had taken his guitar. Pinned to his bedroom door was a message. The only legible words were "Dear Dad," and "peace," and "death."

Chapter 21

O'HARA RETURNED from Montreal on November 5 and I met her at the Marin County heliport with the news that her son had been arrested again and was now missing. From then on we went to bed every night expecting another call from another police department—or from a coroner. O'Hara said to me once, "Aren't there times when you find yourself wishing Mark was dead, to get it over with?"

And I, pushed by guilt, periodically got in the car and drove to areas where I thought Mark might be living, or dying. I tried the Tenderloin, the Haight-Ashbury, and North Beach in San Francisco. I tried Muir Beach, Stinson Beach, and Lagunitas in Marin County. I tried Berkeley. Nothing.

Then on November 20 we did get our middle-of-the-night phone call, but it was not from the police. It was from Pennell, who was sharing a Sausalito house with

two young men we knew and liked. Mark had showed
up. He'd had some sort of scrap with Frank Silvey, one of
Pennell's housemates, and then left again. It was three
in the morning. I cruised the streets around Pennell's
house for a while and saw no one.

The next day Frank told us about it. He had come
home from his job at the No Name Bar at 2:30 A.M.
and found Mark in the kitchen, gobbling sauerkraut from
a can and pacing up and down. Frank asked him to leave,
Mark accused Frank of giving Pennell Methedrine, and
there was a noisy argument. Mark took off his shoes,
struck "some kind of weird karate stance," and screamed,
"I'll kill you. I'll cut your throat."

Frank, a former Marine, started forward but then
restrained himself; Mark, muttering threats and talking
to himself, picked up his guitar and left.

"It was ridiculous," Frank said, "but it was sad, too.
He was spaced way out on dope—I suppose it was speed
—and I could tell by the way he was standing that he
couldn't really fight. But if he's on the street now he's in
danger. If he made a threat like that to some of those
hard-core pushers who hang out on Bridgeway, he'd get
wiped out. They don't fool around."

I called Barney Dreyfus. We agreed that if at all
possible we should get Mark into a hospital for his own
protection. But first we had to find him.

I saw him that afternoon. He was walking rapidly on
Bridgeway, he had a red rag tied Indian-fashion around
his hair, he was wearing a tasseled leather jacket, and I
was certain he was loaded with speed. He was completely
wasted. He tried to avoid me, but I persuaded him to stop.

"I understand you visited Pennell's house the other
night and frightened her."

"Didn't frighten her. Ran into a Meth freak."

"Frank's not a Meth freak, Mark. I know him and he
isn't. If anybody's a Meth freak, it's you."

"I'm a *guitarist*."

"How did you find out where Pennell lived?"

"I dunno."

"Well, I don't want you bothering her. Stay away, you hear?"

"I don't want to talk to you. I'm gonna get a cup of coffee."

"I'll buy coffee for you."

He agreed to go with me to a nearby cafeteria. When I brought two mugs of coffee to our table he held out a dime—his way of showing his financial independence.

"I'll pay for it, Mark. I'm surprised you've got any money. How do you do it?"

"I dunno."

"Are you hustling?"

"No, I'm not hustling."

"Where are you living?"

"With Abby."

"Who's Abby?"

"She's my girl friend. She's beautiful."

He was so taut it was painful to be near him. It was like being near a steel wire that is being pulled tighter and tighter and is going to snap and hurt you. I tried to warn him of the danger involved in threatening strangers. He jumped up and walked outside. I followed, and for a few seconds we leaned against a truck in front of the cafeteria.

"Mark, you seem terribly paranoid to me. I really think the best thing for you would be a hospital."

"I'm paranoid because I hate you."

"OK, you can hate me if you like. But that doesn't mean you shouldn't be in a hospital."

He turned and faced me, staring straight into my eyes.

"I hate you. You want to know why? Because you fucked me and beat me and whipped me."

He wheeled and walked away. As he left I felt my right arm draw back and my fist clench, getting ready to swing at him. I didn't.

Barney Dreyfus and I met twice with Ernest Zunino, an assistant district attorney, to try to piece together a plan that would get Mark off the street and into a hospital, and that would resolve his legal troubles. Zunino seemed anxious to do what was best for Mark. One thing that these meetings proved to me was that California laws on narcotics and hospital commitments are a thicket of contradictions. Even the attorneys seemed to lose their way, and I was hopelessly confused. In the end it was decided that I should go back to the Mental Health Center.

I got an appointment with Dr. James Blevins, a psychiatrist at the Center, who was sympathetic and helpful but not very optimistic at first. He said recent changes in the laws were designed to guarantee that no one could be "railroaded" into an institution. "Mr. Chapin, it's pretty hard to put a man in a state hospital these days just because he's crazy," Dr. Blevins said. He was not being entirely facetious.

Dr. Blevins asked if I could support an affidavit saying that Mark was a danger to himself or to others. I said that on the basis of Mark's threat to Frank Silvey I could and I would, and right then and there I signed a petition that ultimately would produce a court order calling for Mark's apprehension. He would be taken to the Community Mental Health Center for three days of "evaluation," after which a commitment hearing would be held. I made it plain to Dr. Blevins that we wanted Mark committed to Mendocino State Hospital, where he had responded to treatment before, and not to Napa State Hospital. Dr. Blevins assured me it would be Mendocino.

Now the legal machinery had been set in motion. A sheriff's deputy came to our door to pick up Mark. He had the order, signed November 26 by Superior Court Judge Joseph Wilson, the same judge who had committed Mark to Napa two years before. It did not seem as if we had made much progress.

We told the sheriff's deputy Mark was not home, but that he had been seen recently in Sausalito. We asked him to give a copy of the order to the Sausalito police.

And so, at 10:30 P.M. on Decmber 10, while O'Hara and I were watching television, the call we had been waiting for came, from the campus police at the University of California in Berkeley.

"Is this Mr. William Chapin?"

"Yes."

"You have a son, Mark Chapin, age twenty?"

"Yes."

"Well, this is the University of California campus police. Now I want to emphasize, Mr. Chapin, your son is not under arrest. But we do have him in custody here, and if you come over we can release him to you. He was wandering around the campus, seemed pretty confused. Some of the time he wanted to go to the Free Church. Seems like he's been living there. But some of the time he wanted to go home."

I explained the legal situation. I said it would be better for the Marin Sheriff's Department to take him to the Community Mental Health Center. I said I would notify the department right away.

"Well, I hope you do it pretty fast, Mr. Chapin, because I'm off duty in ten minutes. Oh, by the way, we *do* have a record of one arrest of your son by the Berkeley police. December 5. Under the influence of narcotics."

"First I've known about it. He hasn't been home much. How'd he get out of jail?"

"Somebody must have bailed him out."

"It wasn't me."

"Well, *somebody* did."

We left that question up in the air. The important thing was to get Mark into the Mental Health Center. It wasn't going to be easy. It was never easy.

I talked to the Marin Sheriff's Department. A man with a cheery homespun voice said they had no warrant, so they couldn't go across the bay to pick up Mark. I talked to the Sausalito Police Department. The sergeant

on the desk said they had the judge's order all right, but
he couldn't spare the manpower to go over to Berkeley.
Wouldn't the next morning do?

I said I wanted to keep Mark out of a jail cell if I
could. The sergeant phoned the UC police, then got back
to me. "Everything's all set," he said. "They're going to
take Mark to Herrick City Hospital and hold him overnight. We'll get him in the morning."

To the sergeant I said, "Thank you very much." To
O'Hara I said, "Let's have a drink."

We were fifteen minutes into our drinks, good stiff
ones, when a woman who identified herself as the physician in charge at Herrick City Hospital called. "We don't
have an empty bed here, Mr. Chapin. You'll have to come
and get him."

"I'm not even sure he'd go with me," I said. "He was
very hostile the last time I saw him. What would be the
alternative if I didn't come get him?"

"We'd send him to Napa."

"You couldn't take him straight to Marin Community
Mental Health Center? That's where he's supposed to be."

"No, Mr. Chapin, we could not." She was impatient;
she sounded annoyed by the task of talking to a stupid
parent late at night. "No, under the law we'd have to take
him to Napa on a seventy-two-hour hold."

"Is Mark available right now? Let me talk to him."

"Hello, Dad."

"Hello, Mark. How are you?"

"Fine."

I hadn't heard his voice for days. He sounded tired,
subdued, defeated—but in touch. As gently as I could,
glossing over the legal aspects, I said we had arranged
for him to be admitted to the Mental Health Center, and
that he could get treatment there.

"I'm in total agreement," he said.

O'Hara wanted to go with me, but I asked her to stay
home. It would be simpler with two sets of taut emotions

in the car rather than three. I told her to alert the Mental
Health Center.

It was raining and the highways were slick. I crossed
the Golden Gate Bridge and the Oakland Bay Bridge and
arrived at Herrick Hospital before midnight. Mark was in
the emergency section. He stood up and shook hands. I
doubt that he had had a bath in a month. The red rag
he had been wearing on his head protruded from a pants
pocket. His fly was unbuttoned. His hands shook.

A nurse bustled up to us and said, "You're Mr.
Chapin? Your wife just called and said they wouldn't take
him at the Marin Center. I don't know what the problem
is. Sit down and the doctor will talk to you as soon as she's
free."

I sat down. I was drained. Mark said he didn't know
why he had been picked up on the UC campus, he wasn't
doing anything. Of course not. Then O'Hara called back.
"It's all straightened out, love. Take him there, but stop
at the Sausalito police station on the way and get the
papers. I'll tell you about it later."

Mark smelled so bad I kept the car windows open as
we drove back. We didn't try to talk much. We were met
at the Sausalito police station by Sergeant Tom Zink, who
greeted Mark warmly, said he was sorry for what he had
to do, and handed him a copy of the judge's order.

"According to the law, Mark, you're required to read
it," Zink said. "Please read it."

Mark glanced at the paper, squinted strangely, and
put it on the counter.

"No, Mark, you keep it. That's your copy."

Mark was driven to the hospital in a patrol car, behind the wire screen. I followed. We went seventy miles
an hour. "That was a weird ride," Mark said when we
arrived.

They were expecting us. A pretty woman accepted the
papers from the police officer and said, "Mm, they're not
so old"—a remark that made no sense to me until I had
talked to O'Hara. "Everything's fine," the woman said.

Over several 2 A.M. drinks O'Hara told me of the go-around she'd had with the Marin Community Mental Health Center. She had talked to Dr. Benjamin Lee, the doctor on duty in the ward. He had said he wouldn't admit Mark.

"But we have papers saying he's to be admitted for evaluation," O'Hara said to Dr. Lee.

"The law's been changed."

"But the papers were taken out only ten days ago."

"Why didn't you bring the boy in then?"

"We couldn't. We didn't know where he was."

"Well, those papers are obsolete. They aren't any good after twenty-four hours. You'll have to take them out again."

"Dr. Lee, the papers originated right there in your hospi—"

"You're not *listening* to me, Mrs. Chapin. You—are—not—listening."

"But what can we do?"

"You can bring him in tomorrow and he can admit himself on a voluntary basis. He can get outpatient treatment with Dr. Liikane."

O'Hara, in despair and in tears, pleaded with Dr. Lee to reconsider.

"Madame, this conversation is not productive and is not going to become productive." And he hung up.

That was when O'Hara tried to get me at Herrick Hospital, but I hadn't arrived. Then she called the Sausalito police, and fortunately, Sergeant Zink had come on duty. Zink said, "Dr. Lee may be a fine psychiatrist but he doesn't know the law. Those papers are absolutely legal. I'll talk to him."

Zink called the good doctor, and the good doctor backed down.

After Mark was admitted to the Mental Health Center it was as if he had been swallowed up by the earth. I should have phoned the Center, but I was so tired of the whole mess that I didn't. I assumed the Center would phone me. I told Barney I was going to let them make the first move, and he said, "Sure, it's up to them now."

We heard nothing—from the Center, from Mark, from the court. Christmas was approaching. We *had* to know where Mark would be for Christmas. On December 22, while O'Hara was out of the house, I phoned the Center. A nurse came on the line.

"Mr. Chapin, your son was transferred to Napa yesterday."

"Napa! For Christ's *sake!* That wasn't supposed to happen."

"I wouldn't know about that, Mr. Chapin."

"You'd think someone would at least let me know. This is the first I've heard about it."

"You'll have to talk to Dr. Lee about it. You can catch him in the morning before his rounds."

O'Hara came into the house just as I was hanging up. "Mark's in Napa," I said.

She started to cry. She continued to cry, off and on, for the rest of the day and late into the night. Once, when I was holding her, trying to comfort her, she said, "I keep thinking maybe it's going to get a little better and that's just *stupid* because it just gets worse and worse."

I called Napa in the morning and talked to Dr. Kenneth Haworth. He said Mark was all right, but confused and amnesiac. In the course of our talk, I said Mark had responded to Stelazine while he was in Langley Porter.

"Oh, he did, eh?" Dr. Haworth said. "We'll put him on Stelazine, then. See what happens."

I called Barney, who was outraged. I asked him to please see if he could negotiate a transfer to Mendocino State Hospital. I said I was at the end of my rope.

The afternoon mail contained a letter from Mark. It said:

Dear Dad:
    I feel you should know that I am in Napa Hospital and that I am was "on" a 72 hour hold and I would like you to

come and get me from this hole and I hope you are strong enough.

It was unsigned, but every word was legible.

I didn't visit Mark immediately. I felt I had to build some strength for that. I wrote to him, saying his transfer to Napa was a mistake and we were trying to get him moved to Mendocino, but he would have to be patient. He wrote me almost daily. His letters, like this one mailed in January, 1970, were cries for help:

Dear Dad:

I want to go to Mendocino as soon as possible because there is no therapy in Napa and it is supposed to be a 72-hour hold anyway and I know I am in here for drugs rather than being crazy. P.S. Send someone in the family as soon as possible to see me.

Love, Mark

I got a bill from Marin General Hospital for $796.10. It was my first communication with the hospital, and there was no cover letter, no explanation of the move to Napa. I got a bill from an ambulance company for $85, the price of taking Mark up to Napa. I paid the ambulance company. I didn't pay the hospital, which never sent another bill.

The administration at Mendocino told Barney Dreyfus that a transfer should be easy. All it required was a referral from a doctor at the Marin Community Mental Health Center.

Barney talked by phone with Dr. Liikane, of the Health Center. He went into considerable detail, stressing that Mark had wanted to go to Mendocino and that his parents wanted him to go to Mendocino.

"Will you give us the referral, please, Dr. Liikane?"

"No."

"Well, Dr. Liikane. Is that all you're going to say? Aren't you going to tell me why?"

"If you had asked me why, I would tell you why."

"All right, I'm asking you why."

"It was our judgment the patient could be treated better at Napa than at Mendocino."

And that was that. Barney, after describing his conversation with Dr. Liikane, said, "Goddammit, I guess we'll have to take them to court."

He filed suit. Before the suit could be heard, an attorney for the Health Center phoned Barney and said, "Isn't there some way we can settle this out of court?"

"Sure. Send the boy to Mendocino."

"That shouldn't be hard to arrange."

It wasn't hard to arrange. It was arranged with a brisk speed that startled us. Two days later I drove to Napa to take Mark farther north to Mendocino. The ward attendants had his belongings packed, and they gave me his pills in little envelopes. Barney's suit had made the newspapers and our situation was not unknown. We had achieved a minor notoriety, which may have been responsible for our better service.

Mark looked pretty good. He was shaved and his hair was short and his clothes were clean, as if he'd been got ready for a party. He was very glad to see me.

"Hi, Dad," he said, "give me a hug, will you?"

We embraced, and I hid my face in his shoulder so he wouldn't see the tears.

By the end of the day, another long, long day with Mark, he was safely lodged in Mendocino State Hospital. It was where he had to be.

Epilogue

January, 1971

WHEN I BEGAN this family narrative Mark was not yet twenty-one years old. On August 5, 1970, he had his twenty-first birthday. Chronologically, he became a man. Legally, he became his own responsibility.

But in Mark's world this change of estate has only limited meaning. A few days ago while we were walking together he said to me, "There aren't many adults in mental hospitals." I knew what he meant, exactly what he meant, and that he was right—even though the wards of mental hospitals are populated by ancient, gaunt, toothless shadows. Not long after that, when I was sitting alone in the sun outside the cafeteria at Mendocino State Hospital, waiting for Mark to finish his lunch, I was approached by one of those shadows. He looked to be eighty-five. "I was eighteen when I went nuts," he said, and giggled and ambled away. Yes, Mark was right; this old man was *still* eighteen.

And Mark is still at Mendocino. When I drove him up there he was assigned to his old ward, RT-1, but he has moved or been moved from one ward to another, like a boat in search of a good harbor.

Once he was put into a small, experimental group of "emotionally disturbed drug addicts," a category that would seem to include a multitude of problems. The therapeutic emphasis in this group was on daily encounter sessions, rather like those in The Family, and on behavioral discipline. It was supposed to be less rough than The Family. They made Mark wear white cotton gloves to remind him not to pick his nose. He didn't like that at all. It was not in keeping with his dignity, which he has in large measure, and he didn't stay in that group for more than a month or so.

It has taken me a while to do it, but I have learned a lesson: that there is no relationship whatsoever between craziness and dignity. Many of the crazies have more dignity than the non-crazies. It was Mark more than anyone who taught me this, by investing the word with a different set of values. The dignified person will never deliberately hurt or ridicule another person regardless of his station in life. Cruelty is undignified, craziness isn't.

At this writing Mark is a resident of Ward K. It is a quiet ward. Not a great deal is going on there. The patients exist, they have a lot of freedom, as freedom is defined in a mental hospital. Mark plays the records we bring him, and strums his guitar, and at least twice a week resolves to stop smoking, and roams the hospital grounds but does not go beyond them. The fact that not a great deal is going on is a form of therapy. For Mark, it seems to be better therapy than white cotton gloves. He is not as restless, or as anxious.

For a few weeks he read a paperback edition of the Bible. It was the first interest he had shown in organized Christianity since his brief exposure to the Christian Science Church. Then he abruptly stopped reading the Bible, and when I asked him why he said, "I've coughed up God."

Mark is a voluntary patient now, because he is twenty-one years old. He can discharge himself from Mendocino Hospital whenever he wants to.

A week after his twenty-first birthday Mark did discharge himself. A young psychiatric social worker phoned us to say that he had tried to persuade Mark to stay and had failed. So he had no choice but to let him go. "I'm sorry, Mr. Chapin," said the social worker.

Mark put most of his worldly goods into a dirty pillow-case, walked to Ukiah, the city nearest the hospital, and boarded a bus headed south. He went to the Marin County Community Mental Health Center. I am not sure of what happened there, since the Center and I are not on the best of terms; but apparently a well-meaning psychiatrist told Mark that he could live at home and be treated as an out-patient. Late that night, in response to a phone call, I drove to the Mental Health Center and picked up my son. He was standing in the reception room of the main hospital, the pillowcase slung over his shoulder. He was very frightened. I think he was mostly frightened of me.

"I tried to get a baby-sitter job," he said to me as we drove down the highway toward Sausalito.

"Oh? How'd you do that?"

"I bought a newspaper and looked up some ads and phoned some people."

"Have any luck?"

"No. They didn't want me, I guess."

"Where'd you get the money to do all this?"

"I had a dollar."

The poor crazy bastard. He had a dollar, a lousy *dollar*, and enough guts to try to get a baby-sitter job. For Mark, it must have been an act of supreme courage and determination just to read the classified-ad section. To read it and try to make sense out of it.

And I knew then why he had left the hospital. He had

turned twenty-one, he had come of age; he thought O'Hara and I might abandon him and he would have to support himself, because he was twenty-one.

Mark slept in his own bed that night, and the following morning O'Hara and a very close friend who works with autistic children drove him back to the hospital. He did not resist. Under the law, the hospital was not compelled to readmit him, but Mendocino's medical director is a compassionate man, and Mark was readmitted.

Mark has been home for weekend visits. He is quiet and cooperative, and the visits have gone well. We do not leave him in the house alone for more than a few minutes. He complains about his hallucinations, calling them "a private hell," and he never talks of running away from the hospital.

During a recent visit O'Hara and I took him to another psychiatrist, Dr. James F. Donovan, who has a private practice in Marin County and who acts as a consultant to our friend who works with autistic children. It was she who urged us to see him. I was by no means certain of what I hoped to achieve, and neither was Dr. Donovan; but he was quite willing to give us an appointment, and all three of us—O'Hara, Mark, and I—liked him immediately. That in itself was an achievement.

Dr. Donovan's waiting room was small and cubelike, and Mark said it reminded him of Sartre's *No Exit*.

The doctor talked with Mark alone, and then talked with O'Hara and me while Mark sat in the waiting room.

"What do you want me to say?" he asked us.

"What do you think of him?"

"I think he's got the disease all right. He's acutely ill."

I did not have to ask—I knew beyond any doubt that the disease Dr. Donovan referred to was schizophrenia, and that Mark had it bad. The word had been used in connection with Mark before; but always, I think, I had refused to give the word its full weight, had shoved it aside. But now the word came from a man whom I in

stinctively trusted, and I could no longer shove it aside.
I had to accept it.

Besides, I was tired of self-deception. I had been running away, just as Mark ran away.

Dr. Donovan went on to say that Mark impressed him
as a person who had been schizophrenic for a number of
years; that there was always the "remote possibility of
spontaneous remission"; that Mark's hallucinations were
actually a hopeful sign because they represented his
struggle against total, catatonic withdrawal; that Mark
had quite sharp insights about his condition; that the hospital was by far the best place for him now; and that
Mark, in his view, might very well have become schizophrenic even if he had never taken drugs.

The question of brain damage did not arise. We had
enough to ponder without going into that.

"You must be up to your neck with suggestions of
what to do about Mark," Dr. Donovan said, and then, almost apologetically, he offered some suggestions, pointed
to a few more avenues for us to explore. All of them
seemed worthwhile. We thanked him and left. I was relieved to find that Mark had not wandered away from the
little room that reminded him of Sartre's *No Exit*. Perhaps
he felt powerless to do so.

When the three of us got to the car, it was dark, and
there came upon me a great flood of feeling, so great that
it was beyond pain or grief or hate or love. It was the
feeling that Mark would be with O'Hara and me until we
died. It would make no difference whether he got better
or got worse or even died. He was part of us, he emerged
from us, he would be with us forever; it was as simple as
that.

"I'm going to study the guitar when I get to England,"
Mark said as he climbed into the back seat of the car and
I closed the door. We drove home.

What went wrong? We search endlessly for answers,
and endlessly we are turned back.

It seems to me it should be obvious that I do not know what went wrong, and neither do the doctors. The doctors can help, they can alleviate, they can exercise certain controls, they can look carefully and deeply into a million minds; but they cannot say, for sure, what went wrong. The good ones cannot, that is.

Of all the people whom I have met in the field of mental health, the one I admire the most is Dr. Norman Garmezy, the University of Minnesota psychologist. I have the highest regard for his intelligence and his humanity; but more than that, he is a dear friend. Norman has spent an academic lifetime on research into the causes of schizophrenia; but so far, he said to me recently, he does not truly *know* what the causes are. He is still trying to discover them, and will continue to try until he retires.

So this book becomes, in the words of a perceptive newspaperman who read the manuscript, "an existential story that may or may not help to illuminate a mad world."

If Mark should get well, if he should have "a spontaneous remission," or if one psychiatrist succeeds where others have failed, or if the scientists should find a cure for schizophrenia, then I will write a book about his recovery. Or better, Mark himself will write the book because he, far more than I, should be able to describe how he has suffered, and tell why he stopped suffering.

But O'Hara and I do not count on this happening. Neither have we given up hope.

Meanwhile, I can guess, I can suggest.

I think that heredity may have more to do with it than environment. It is easier to blame environment, and that can lead one astray. A persuasive argument can be made that Mark, through his heredity on my side of the family, was born with a predisposition toward mental illness. Several decades ago mental illness was something *other* people had; and it was kept hidden, behind shuttered windows. What the people in my family had was "eccentricity," which was not only condoned, it was often admired. I think rightfully so; everyone shouldn't be like everyone else.

But was it always just eccentricity? When I was a child I heard one of my mother's brothers referred to as "brilliant," "unpredictable," and "a smart aleck." Indeed he was brilliant: when he was eight years old he wrote a full-length novel about a cat. His mind was an encyclopedia. As a child I was often compared with him, and I deeply resented it. I did not want to have his smart-aleck traits. I now believe that this man, my uncle, who left society to embrace a series of esoteric religions, was eventually a schizophrenic. A parallel can be drawn between his intellectual precocity and Mark's.

Another uncle, a professor at the University of Vermont and one of the nicest of men, committed suicide at a relatively early age.

My father's father spent years in a mental institution, and died there. He had to be "put away," as the expression used to go. Within the family, it was never discussed. I can't even remember how I first heard about it, or when.

When my sister had her emotional breakdown at the end of World War II, she went to Montreal to receive expensive treatment, and she recovered.

And what about me? I cannot count the number of times I have blacked out from drinking too much, the number of times I have arrived at a stage where all I wanted to do was pour booze down my throat. I have been a danger to myself and, behind the wheel of an automobile, a danger to others. Ten years ago I would have sworn that I never had a hallucination. Now I know I have had several. Yet I have always managed to function reasonably well as a social being. I have never gone over the brink.

As I write this, it sounds too much like exhibitionism. Here we are, the crazy Chapins with all their frailties! Exposing all the things that are supposed to be hidden lest someone be embarrassed! But damn it, keeping them hidden hasn't accomplished much. The world's a nutty place. Maybe if we (and by "we" I mean a great many people) stop trying to keep our frailties hidden and stop being ashamed of things we cannot change, the scientists and the doctors *will* discover the causes of schizophrenia, and a cure for it.

And what a blessing that would be; not only for the Mark Chapins of the world, but for everyone.

Having suggested that heredity has more to do with mental illness than environment, I must still ask, "Why did Mark go under and Pennell survive?" They had the same parents, the same heredity.

Again, I do not know. I can only guess that it is a random disease, that it chooses random victims. The evidence appears to bear this out. Mental hospitals are crammed with long-term patients who are visited by their healthy brothers and sisters. The superintendent of Napa State Hospital once told me that "schizophrenia touches every family," but he would not have tried to predict which one member of a family schizophrenia would strike down and which spare.

Besides, opinions vary, and are contradictory. Some opinions do put environment firmly into the picture. One psychologist has suggested that our family structure— strong mother, weak father—was a much heavier burden on Mark than it was on Pennell—because there was no one Mark could easily identify with as he grew up. Another psychologist said just the opposite, that O'Hara was weak and I strong.

I myself think that O'Hara and I both have our strengths and weaknesses, and that it is risky to over-simplify. We did what we did. We could have done better —or worse. I think we would have been doing better had we been more consistent with our children. Children very much need that consistency, that steadiness. If they are uncertain how their mother or father is going to react to a family incident—laughter? praise? anger? love?

indifference?—they will be uncertain when they leave the family. Or perhaps they will never leave.

A family should be a large, steadily flowing river; the water parts before unyielding obstacles and then comes together again. It is constant. But not many families are like that, and ours wasn't.

Which brings us, in a less than perfect circle, back to the question: what went wrong?

I have one final guess. Granted Mark's susceptibility to mental illness, the single factor that damaged him more than any other was my inability to express love, my inability to tell him outright that I loved him. I have always been able to *feel* love for others, but what good does it do if it is not expressed?

Once, during World War II, I watched silently in a New York subway station while a short, fat, Jewish father said goodby to his son, who was a gunner on my bomber crew. We were scheduled to go overseas the next day. Father and son held each other and kissed each other and said they loved each other. It was beautiful, and there was no room for doubt, and I watched with a feeling close to envy. Because we Chapins never did that.

Now, years later, it is almost as though Mark *had* to get sick because this was the only way he could make me express my love for him. If this is true, then his sickness is a kind of gift, for it is a terrible thing not to be able to express love.

I no longer work for the San Francisco *Chronicle*. I still have many friends there. But I was fed up with the night hours and the petty frustrations that are inescapable in the newspaper business, and I inherited some money, enough to make it easy to quit.

I loafed for a while. Then I began teaching full time in the Journalism Department at San Francisco State College. I am not sure journalism is what I teach, but I enjoy telling young people about newspapers and the men and women who work on newspapers. I seem to get along very well with my students, and they get along very well with me.

And I wrote this book, which I like to think of as an expression of my love for my son Mark. Some day he will know that it is.

GARDNER WEBB COLLEGE LIBRARY